SERMONETTES, ILLUSTRATIONS, AND PRAYERS
FROM
A
UNITED METHODIST COUNTRY PREACHER

Volume Two

SERMONETTES, ILLUSTRATIONS, AND PRAYERS
FROM
A
UNITED METHODIST COUNTRY PREACHER

* * * * *

A Pathway to the Development of Christlike Behavior
Volume Two

* * * * *

*For God so loved the world, that He gave His one
and only Son, that whoever believes in Him shall
not perish but have eternal life.*
- John 3:16

* * * * *

Prepared by
The Holy Spirit of God
and
Reverend Leslie "Les" Goode

Published by Leslie Goode

Williamsburg, Virginia

Copyright © 2021 by Leslie Goode

ISBN: 978-1-7365778-1-3 (paperback)

ISBN: 978-1-7365778-2-0 (eBook)

TABLE OF CONTENTS

Introduction

The format for this compilation consists of Sermonettes, Illustrations, and Prayers. The illustrations hopefully illuminate the topics of the shortened messages which in turn will invite you to each closing prayer. As the illustrations are read, be prepared to see yourself in many of them. A sermonette may be viewed by some as Spirit-driven, for somebody else. In such a case, maybe after the prayer, the sermonette should be read once again. As to the prayers, each one should be read first before praying. Make notes on the pages as the Holy Spirit crafts the words to become your personal prayer. Use the listed prayers as guides to enhance your talks with God.

One final point, it will assist you greatly to read first the Scripture references cited with each of the sermonettes.

It is my prayer that God, through the Holy Spirit and Jesus the Christ, will use this book to strengthen you on your earthly spiritual journey and further prepare you for your eternal, heavenly home. As you read, be prepared—you might just feel some surprises coming your way!

The Lord's Prayer

Our Father, who art in heaven,
Hallowed be Thy name.
Thy kingdom come,
Thy will be done on earth as it is in heaven.
Give us this day our daily bread,
And forgive us our trespasses,
As we forgive those who trespass against us.
And lead us not into temptation,
But deliver us from evil.
For thine is the Kingdom, and the power,
And the glory forever. Amen.

The Season of Christmas and Hope

SERMONETTE

Isaiah 40:31

The season in the Protestant Church called Advent is a time to search our hearts as we prepare for Christmas. Time to prepare for the greatest gift ever received—God coming to us in the physical form of a baby! It's during this season (four weeks) that we decide which of the two Christmases we want to spend most of our time celebrating.

A little boy was asked, "Did you get all you wanted at Christmas?"

"No," he replied and added, "But that's okay because it's not my birthday."

Christmas is not only a time for giving but is also a time for receiving, and Advent prepares us for this. In all the presents, food, and fellowship, we have the opportunity to receive blessings from God. So, we have a choice as to how much time we spend on the two Christmases—the first, the spiritual impact of the birth of Jesus the Christ, and the second, the visit from the worldly Santa Claus.

It's not one or the other, but rather how much time is spent on each one. We can have a Christmas of the heart and receive hope, peace, joy, love, etc. We can also spend our time running around town trying to find the perfect gift for Aunt Matilda, which she won't like or use anyway!

In the season of Advent, we are preparing for the great gift from God—the way to salvation (deliverance from sin). But we can get so caught up in the Christmas of the world that we can overlook the Christmas present we received from God. Advent calls us to a conscious decision concerning our relationship with God through the birth, life, death, and resurrection of Jesus. Having accepted Jesus as Lord and Savior, we have a personal relationship with God which allows us the opportunity to accept God's gifts—hope, trust, spiritual growth, calmness in a crisis, etc. But you don't have to accept them; just because you get a new shirt doesn't mean you have to wear it!

Lord Ruth of English nobility once said, "I do not like a crisis, but I do like the opportunities they provide!"

In Advent, we come to realize that in a crisis, our cry should be, "Wait until you see what God does through my gifts and God's gifts, including the gift of the Holy Spirit."

Remember, you don't have to accept your gift; you can try and do it alone (satan loves this decision!). I believe that Advent tells all Christians they should be optimists (although not all optimists are Christian). The pessimist always expects the worst—that evil outweighs good, that no good deed goes unpunished.

In this season, the expectation of what is to come brings to us a sense of hope. Christians should always fall back on hope—even though it looks grim, it will be interesting (even exciting) to see what God does with that *thing*. And you will find that you have gifts and talents given to you, and you didn't even know you had them, mainly because you weren't listening and have not used them. Even though you don't see a clear answer and there are twists and turns in the journey, when you travel with God in hope and faith, there are no dead ends! Hope knows that God has a path, and it might not be the path you preferred. If your hope begins to wane, maybe you are holding on to the wrong thing and are not listening to God who is trying to redirect you.

You can keep on asking God for the red Ferrari, but chances are overwhelming you won't get it! Doesn't mean you won't get a car but be prepared as God does show many times a sense of humor. During Advent, you can learn to pray for spiritual gifts, such as Wisdom, Knowledge, Faith, Service, Teaching, Administration,

Leadership, and Showing Mercy. You can also pray for the ability to identify and use all the gifts given to you by God. Advent invites you to a closer relationship with God through hope.

Two Christmases—how much time are you going to devote to each one this year?

ILLUSTRATIONS

As a young man, I attended a small, country church located not far from my house. The congregation seemed very friendly, but that was about to change due to a situation on the church grounds.

Some members noticed the big, historical tree between the parking lot and the sidewalk was dying. The decaying of the inner core was determined to be irreversible. Many of the newer members wanted it cut down immediately before it fell on the cars or on somebody. Many older members wanted to wait and give it time as they reminisced over such things as the color of the leaves in the fall and climbing the tree limbs many years ago. One couple had been married under the tree limbs.

The church became divided between a *hazard* and an *old friend*. Feelings were hurt, and church council meetings became loud and accusatory. Some members threatened to leave the church if the tree wasn't cut down, and some threatened to leave if it was cut down. Then, God called on nature to settled the matter, and a strong wind early in the morning hours toppled the tree.

The problem was solved, but I remember thinking, "How could a church, where Jesus Christ is the head, almost split over a dying tree?"

Maybe the church was not as strong spiritually as I thought, and maybe it was dying also.

A healthy church knows that Jesus is the head, and everyone seeks to find His will, especially in times of disagreement. This also is true in our individual lives. We should know that Jesus is the head of our life and always seek to find His will. The tree might have been saved if action had been taken earlier—how about your soul?

Following Christ will revitalize your soul and lead you away from soul-shattering experiences, no matter how pleasant they may first appear. Jesus is the head of your life; do you consider Him a hazard or an old friend? It can't be both, with jumping back and forth between the two. It's time to take care of your soul now, before it's in Christ's presence.

* * * * *

It was just a few days before Christmas. Two men who were next-door neighbors decided to go sailing while their wives went Christmas shopping. While the men were out in their sailboat, a storm arose. The sea became very angry, and the men had great difficulty keeping the boat under control. As they maneuvered their way toward the land, they hit a sandbar, and the boat grounded. Both men jumped overboard and began to push and shove with all their strength, trying to get the boat into deeper water. With his feet almost knee-deep in mud, and the waves bouncing him against the side of the boat, and his hair blowing wildly in the rain-filled wind, one of the men said, "Boy, this is bad, *but* it sure beats shopping!"

* * * * *

I hope your Christmas Day was a success—good food, gifts, family. After all the maddening preparations, the day passed rather quickly. And now we have memories and stories.

As one lady said to her husband, "Next year, why don't we give only sensible gifts to each other, like ties and a mink coat."

A woman was telling her friend about Christmas at her house. "I was visited by a jolly fellow with a big bag over his shoulder; my son came home from college with his dirty laundry."

Santa has gone back to the North Pole leaving most of us with debt. On the other hand, what has the birth story left you with this year?

* * * * *

An old pioneer traveled westward across the great plains of our country until he came to an abrupt halt at the edge of the Grand Canyon. He gawked at the sight before him—a vast chasm one mile deep, eighteen miles across, more than one hundred miles long. He gasped, "Something must have happened here."

A visitor to our world at Christmas time, seeing the lights, decorations, the trees, parades, religious services, would probably say, "Something must have happened here!"

Indeed, something did happen; God came to our world on that first Christmas. Are you ready to believe and surrender to that event, if you have not already done so? Blessings abound for those who do.

PRAYER

Faithful and ever-present God, I open my heart to You to pay allegiance to You as the One who is always true in my life. There are other false gods who have vied for my attention this past week. If my attention was directed from You, I ask forgiveness and strength to be more vigilant in my search for Your way. Help me to see clearly that the main purpose of the evil one is the undoing of my pursuit of Your great love. For in the false message and lie of my own ability to deal with satan's snares alone, I tend to rely on myself and draw away from Your protection, guidance, and love.

I know I am not able to effectively serve two masters at the same time, and in the haste of the moment, the desire for my will, and the overconfidence in my own ability, I choose to not seek Your counsel. I decide to not peacefully await Your conviction of my heart. Rather than bathe my potential actions in the vastness of Your understanding, I rely on short-sighted goals and possible events and not Your vision. Only to see later that misguided actions would have been avoided if only I had awaited a time with patience in Your name.

You have given to me the gift of Your presence in the Holy Spirit, which is real and active within me. An Advocate, a Comforter, a Presence as close as my next breath. A Friend beyond all other friends. A Force stronger than evil with the ability to see clearly the spiritual path right for me. I am truly not alone. And yet, I act as if I am alone. I fail to embrace the salvation found in the words and actions of Jesus as a model for my life, the strength and endurance of the Holy Spirit with me, and a place in Your eternal home.

Precious God, I thank You for the ever-present Holy Spirit. May I feel that presence, growing stronger in reliance on the message in my spiritual heart, walking more in faith, and trusting the ways of the Holy Spirit. Accept my prayers to You as I seek Your will through the Holy Spirit.

I pray for a spiritual presence in the lives of loved ones and friends, who I name to You, who are sick in mind, body, or spirit. In their challenges, may they feel the Holy Spirit's presence, receive the strength they need, and heal as Your will directs. Even for those so dear to me, my faith allows me to rely on "Thy will be done."

It is my continued prayer that world leaders seek peace, not war; that hearts be turned to service, not power; that freedom becomes a dream come true for all. These things I ask in confidence in the name of Jesus the Christ who taught the prayer saying, "Our Father . . ."

What Do You Hope For?

SERMONETTE

Romans 15:13

If God has our best interest at heart, why don't we always see God's will? One of the impediments is, simply put, how do we know it's God's will?

In Judges 6:36-40, God called a man named Gideon to lead an army, and Gideon was promised victory. To make sure he had it right, Gideon said to God, "If you will save Israel by my hand as you have promised—look, I will place a wool fleece on the threshing floor. If there is dew only on the fleece and all the ground is dry, I will know that you will save Israel by my hand, as you said."

And that is what happened! Then Gideon said to God, "Do not be angry with me. Let me make just one more request. Allow me one more test with the fleece, but this time make the fleece dry and let the ground be covered with dew."

That night, God did so!

Unfortunately, it's not always this clear for us. How do we know God's will? Most of the time we don't know until after the fact. When we have an important decision to make, we want to first present it to God and seek God's will to be made known through wisdom and understanding. We can also seek guidance from Christian men and women for God may use them to bring His answer. We can engage our own system of ethics, morals, and integrity. And, although the answer might still not be crystal clear, when we feel the Holy Spirit giving a sense of direction, we step out in faith.

In following God's will, there is almost always an element of trust in the God who can't lie. But there is one caution for all Christians to be aware of—there might be some levels of trust along the journey before you get to the desired anticipation. Just because you pray and step out in faith doesn't mean the desired situation will come about next week, next month, or even next year.

It might also be true that God has to find a way to convince you that you are on the wrong path. Failure is a good teacher! As concerns your relationship with God, there is always an opportunity in failure. It might be that you are on the right path but have to go through some "adjustments" to fully prepare you for the blessing. But, don't give up—God will lead you to the best solution.

It could also be that you are trying so hard to get your way, it will take a while to figure out God's alternative plan. If you're going to sit around and wait for God to write the answer on the ceiling of your room, you could be in for a long, long wait. And when God writes it on your spiritual heart, it might still feel scary. Step out in faith and enjoy the ride!

It's also true that when we step out in faith, we also step out in hope. Hope is defined as "a desire accompanied by expectation." In the Bible, the psalmist writes, "In His word I put my hope" (Psalm 130:5).

The prophet Isaiah has these words, "Those who hope in the Lord will renew their strength" (Isaiah 40:31).

The Apostle Paul writes in Romans 8:24-25, "Hope that is seen is no hope at all. Who hopes for what they already have? But if we hope for what we do not yet have, we wait for it patiently."

From this, we can conclude that our chances are greater when what we hoped for draws us closer to God and helps the Kingdom of Christ on this earth. God acts unexpectedly also. A mother had the hope that her son would serve God, not crime. He was arrested and sentenced, and her reply was, "Well, maybe God wanted to meet him in prison."

A man prays and hopes his wife would be cancer-free without pain. Maybe God meets her cancer-free in her heavenly home. Hope is our anchor. Be bold. Hope to be more Christlike. Hope that nothing you have will lead you from worshiping God. Hope you will be given opportunities to testify to your faith. Hope you will put more faith and trust in the One who cannot lie. And hope and believe in the resurrection story. Hope is the word that keeps Christians going. What do you hope for?

ILLUSTRATIONS

It seems that a young man was at the end of his rope. Seeing no way out, he dropped to his knees in prayer. "Lord," he said, "I can't go on. I have too heavy a cross to bear."

The Lord appeared in a vision and took him to a large room filled with crosses. And, as they entered the room, the Lord said, "My son, if you cannot bear the weight of your cross, just place your cross inside this room. Then look around and pick out any cross you wish."

The man was filled with relief. "Thank you, Lord," he replied with a sigh, and he did as he was told.

The room was large and contained many crosses. Some so large that the tops weren't even visible. Then he turned around a little corridor and spotted a tiny cross leaning against the wall close to the door. "I'd like that one, Lord," he whispered.

And the Lord replied, "My son, that is the cross you just brought in."

"Take up thy cross and follow me," Jesus said. Are there days or times when your cross of life seems too large and heavy to carry, no matter how big or small it happens to be? Times when you feel overwhelmed or feel yourself drained. A time when even the purpose of it all comes into question. A time when no matter how hard you try, it just won't all come together, and the weight of your burdens pushes you down. The joy of life seems to slip away as you spend your time just getting through the day.

And then when you try and solve your problems, frustration seems to be your reward—like the woman who called the police station to report a skunk in her cellar. The police told her to make a trail of breadcrumbs from the basement to the yard and to wait for the skunk to follow the breadcrumbs.

A little later, the frustrated woman called back and said, "I did what you said. Now I have two skunks in my cellar."

Frustration—heavy burdens of life. And then, into this gray time in the life of a Christian, one little word enters the scene. One little word that begins to drive out the darkness and to bring in the warm sunshine of joy and then strength is renewed. Such a small word, but oh, what a big word.

Hope—a feeling that God will take even this and make something good out of it; that even in this, peace can be ours—and we know in our very being that with God's presence and strength, this too shall pass.

* * * * *

There was once a family that celebrated Christmas every year with a birthday party for Jesus. An extra chair of honor was placed at the table to remind the family of Jesus's presence. The empty chair reminds the Christian of the Christmas hope.

The Christmas hope. The Christmas of the heart. During the weeks before Christmas (Advent), what kind of preparation are you making? It's not Santa Claus's birthday.

Here's a good test—see how many hours you spend cooking, wrapping, buying, etc., and compare this to the number of hours telling the birth story, praying, visiting, etc. Maybe some people hate the Christmas holidays because they are celebrating the wrong Christmas!

* * * * *

Hope is the belief that something is going to realistically happen. If I run and jump off a cliff hoping I will be able to flap my arms and fly, that's not realistic.

Our love of God will be rewarded, but maybe not in the way we had planned. When a person's hope is in the love of God, it can never be an illusion for God loves us with an everlasting love backed by an everlasting power.

The story is told of a couple from Virginia who purchased a huge RV to travel across the country and back. Somewhere in the Midwest, they decided to take an off-route road to see the scenery. The RV ended up in a ditch in a very desolate area, and they were stranded (a time well before cell phones).

As days went by without sighting another vehicle, hope, food, and water began to run low. More days went by, and they didn't see how they could be found, and yet through prayer, hope seemed to stay faintly alive.

Then one day, they heard the faint drone of an airplane engine. As it got stronger, their hope was renewed. A little time later, it flew over them, and the pilot dipped the wings to let them know they were sighted. They both agreed that the faint glow of hope kept them alive.

Someone once said, "You can live forty days without food, eight days without water, four minutes without air, but only a few seconds without hope."

The evil one's task is to use trials of the world and temptations to separate us from God by losing hope in the promises and love of God. Is there a situation in your life for which you are beginning to lose hope? Could it be that you are holding on to the wrong thing, and God is trying to redirect you? Could it be God is bringing the answer that you don't want to hear? Could it be the evil one is messing with you?

Hope is found in prayer and often tells us, "Yeah, this looks pretty grim, *but* it's going to be interesting to see what God does with it!"

Remember, when you travel with God, there are no dead ends.

* * * * *

Hope keeps life open to new possibilities. Having accepted Jesus the Christ as our Lord and Savior, we have a personal relationship with God, through Jesus, and when we have trust and patience in God, things that come into our life, even suffering, are lined up to achieve growth and blessings. But, as God's children, we have to supplant our will with God's will—to let go and let God. This builds our hope as our character develops in trust.

Some years ago, at a great university, there was a piano teacher who was simply known as Herman. One night at a university concert, a distinguished guest piano player suddenly became ill while performing an extremely difficult piece. No sooner had the artist been taken from the stage when Herman rose from his seat in the audience, walked on stage, sat down at the piano, and with great mastery, completed the performance.

Later that evening, people who had been in the audience asked Herman how he was able to perform such a demanding piece so beautifully without notice or rehearsal.

He replied, "In 1937 when I was a budding young concert pianist, I was arrested and placed in a Nazi concentration camp. Putting it mildly, the future looked bleak. But something spoke inwardly to me, and I knew that to keep the flicker of hope alive, that I might someday play again, I needed to practice every day.

"I began fingering a piece of the board that was part of my bed one night. The next night I added a second piece and soon I was running through my entire repertoire. I did this every night for five years, for something inside me kept telling me to keep practicing, to have hope.

"It so happens that the piece I played tonight at the concert hall was part of that repertoire. That constant practice is what kept my hope alive. Every day I renewed my hope that I would one day be able to play my music again on a real piano and in freedom."

How is God able to exercise a personal relationship with us that gives us perseverance through pressures of the world, builds our character, and leads us to hope? Can't wait to see, God, what You are going to do next. This situation looks pretty messy, *but* I know You are working on a blessing.

How does God mix and mingle with us as the Holy Spirit? In Romans 5:5, we find our answer. "And hope does not put us to shame, because God's love has been poured out into our hearts through the Holy Spirit, who has been given to us."

The Christian hope never proves to be an illusion, for it is founded on the love of God. What hope have you discussed with God lately?

* * * * *

. . . for hope sees beyond despair; hope sees what can be, even if briefly. Hope oftentimes lets us know that someone cares.

Several years ago, a teacher assigned to work with children in a large hospital received a routine call requesting that she visit a particular child. She took the boy's name and room number and was told by the teacher on the other end of the phone, "We're studying nouns and adverbs in his class now. I'd be grateful if you could help him with his homework so he doesn't fall behind the others."

It wasn't until the visiting teacher got inside the boy's room that she realized it was located in the hospital's burn unit. No one had prepared her to find a young boy horribly burned and in great pain. She felt she couldn't just turn and walk away, so she awkwardly stammered, "I'm the hospital teacher, and your regular teacher sent me to help you with nouns and adverbs."

The next morning a nurse on the burn unit asked her, "What did you do to that boy?"

Before she could finish a profusion of apologies, the nurse interrupted her, "You don't understand. We've been very worried about him, but since you came yesterday, his whole attitude has changed. He's fighting back, responding to treatment . . . It's as though he's decided to live."

The boy explained later that he had completely given up hope until he saw the teacher. It all changed when he realized a simple fact. With joyful tears he explained, "They wouldn't send a teacher to work on nouns and adverbs with a dying boy, now would they?"

Hope says this too shall pass, and it will be used as background for a better day. If you don't know hope, are you sure you have a personal walk with Jesus the Christ?

PRAYER

Dear one and only God, I come in prayer to praise You and give thanks for my many blessings, especially the blessing of family and friends with whom I share life's journey. May they see in me Christlike behavior and be strengthened in their faith journey. For in each of our lives, we will be aware of times of darkness, hurt, and disillusionment; a time when we didn't seem to be able to find our way or even to know if there was a way.

In their presence, I want to be able to testify that You never forsake Your children. Your light of truth and wisdom renews our hope and gives us strength and courage to see the joy of a new and different day. A day of sunshine and rainbows and peacefulness of Spirit.

In order that I may be a faithful witness, help me practice talking all things meaningful over with You. May my faith and trust in You increase and my reliance on self, decrease. Gracious God, I know that during my days, joy and happiness will be found along with sorrow and sadness. But, whatever the season of my life, may I demonstrate faith, and may my first response be, "I have faith and trust in the one true God and confidence the Holy Spirit will lead me into God's vision."

For Your word in Scripture tells me that nothing can separate me from You unless I do it myself. Give me the wisdom to guard against complacency in my relationship with You and always stir up within me Your eternal hope. Hope that trials will be preparation for a better day; hope that my trust will bring peace and quietness of spirit; hope that when my earthly race has been run, that I will stand in Your presence and hear, "Well done, good and faithful servant."

As I travel life's journey, may I be ever more comfortable with You, the Holy Spirit, and the Risen Jesus as my traveling companions. May family members, friends, and others see me strive to live my faith in all I do. May Your hope and peace be a part of all our lives, especially in times of struggle. May even adversity draw all to You.

In this world of violence, war, and terrorism, my hope remains that You will soften the hearts of world leaders drawing them to Your service and Your will.

These things I ask in the name of Jesus, my Redeemer, who taught the prayer saying, "Our Father . . ."

What Do You Plan to Do About It?

SERMONETTE

1 Corinthians 10:11-13

When trials, tribulations, and confusion come into our lives, we can't say they make us happy. We are more likely to ask, "Why me?"

Yet in the New Testament, we find writers who took a different path which, for most people, could be a hard path to follow. For example, in James (one of Jesus's brothers) 1:2-4, he writes, "Consider it pure joy, my brothers and sisters, whenever you face trials of many kinds, because you know that the testing of your faith produces perseverance. Let perseverance finish its work so that you may be mature and complete, not lacking anything."

And in verses 12-15, he continues, "Blessed is the one who perseveres under trial because, having stood the test, that person will receive the crown of life that the Lord has promised to those who love him. When tempted, no one should say, "God is tempting me." For God cannot be tempted by evil, nor does he tempt anyone; but each person is tempted when they are dragged away by their own evil desire and enticed. Then, after desire has conceived, it gives birth to sin; and sin, when it is full-grown, gives birth to death."

James continues with these words. "Don't be deceived, my dear brothers and sisters. Every good and perfect gift is from above, coming down from the Father of the heavenly lights, who does not change like shifting shadows" (James 1:16-17).

Paul, the writer of several New Testament books, writes similarly with the concept of bringing on the hardships! When we pass trials by standing firm in the Word of God and use Christ as our example, we claim and receive our home eternal.

If we look just below these words, we find an answer to the cause of a vast number of the trials and temptations—satan! Satan is always trying to draw us away from God and he entices us in our weaknesses.

Remember the comic strip *Pogo* where he famously said, "We have met the enemy, and it is us!" Remember, being tempted is not a sin (Jesus was tempted in the wilderness). Acting on and accepting temptation is the sin. So we must remember that when the Holy Spirit pricks our conscience which warns us that we are considering or have started a path that violates our moral ethics, it's the devil's doing—not God's. No matter how many excuses are made, the truth remains that when we fall for temptation we are supporting the devil's work!

In 1 Peter 5:8, we read, "Your enemy the devil prowls around like a roaring lion looking for someone to devour." The devil is not stupid but is very relentless. The devil will dress up his temptations to make them so appealing. He will never tell you he desires to separate you from God while stealing your joy and peace. When our conscience tells us we are facing temptation, the best position to take is still to ask yourself, "What would Jesus do?"

In His experience in the wilderness, we can identify Jesus's answer. "Get away from me, satan!" Remember, when satan knocks, let Jesus answer the door. It wouldn't hurt to pray to God for help from the Holy Spirit. We are not as much a victim as we sometimes pretend. "The devil made me do it!"

No. The devil makes his will so appealing that he hopes you will bend your will to his. The question is not *if* you are tempted, but rather *when* you are tempted. Then you will have a choice—live dangerously and play along with satan for immediate satisfaction, or call on God through Jesus and the Holy Spirit. You cannot defeat satan on your own. You don't have to—through faith, you can resist. At the next temptation, what do you plan to do?

ILLUSTRATIONS

Sometimes things get confused. A woman dialed the number of what she thought was the local record shop. A man answered and she asked, "Do you have *Ten Little Fingers and Ten Little Toes in Alabama?*"

The man in the barbershop had no idea what she was talking about. He said, "No, but I do have a wife and fifteen kids in Louisiana."

She asked, "Is that a record?"

He said, "I don't know if it's a record or not, but it sure is above the average!"

Or how about the Italian gentleman who was trying to learn English. He asked an American friend, "What is a polar bear?"

His friend replied that a polar bear lived up north. The Italian asked, "But what does this polar bear do?"

"Well," answered the American, "he sits on a cake of ice and eats raw fish."

"Oh, no," he said. "I will not do it!"

His befuddled American friend asked, "What won't you do?"

The Italian said, "I have just been asked to be a polar bear at a funeral, and I just won't do it!"

Some things are just confusing. Here is one that is not: "For God so loved the world that He gave His one and only Son, that whoever believes in Him shall not perish but have eternal life" (John 3:16).

* * * * *

On June 18, 1815, the Battle of Waterloo took place. The French, under the command of Napoleon, were fighting the allies (British, Dutch, and Germans) under the command of Wellington.

The people of England depended on a system of signaling to find out how the battle was going. One of these signal stations was on the tower of the Winchester Cathedral. Late in the day, it flashed the signal, "Wellington Defeated," just as one of the English fogs moved in and made it impossible to see the sign.

The news of the defeat quickly spread throughout the city. The whole countryside was sad and gloomy when they heard the news that the country had lost the war. Suddenly, the fog lifted, and the whole message could be read. The message had four words, not two. The complete message was, "Wellington Defeated the Enemy."

It only took a few minutes for the good news to spread. Sorrow turned to joy; defeat was turned to victory. So it was when Jesus was laid in the tomb on the first Good Friday. Hope had died even in the hearts of Jesus's most loyal friends. After the crucifixion, the fog of disappointment and misunderstanding crept in on the followers of Jesus. They had read only part of the message. "Christ defeated" was all they could see.

But then, that Easter Sunday, the fog lifted and the world received the complete message—"Christ defeated death." Defeat was turned to victory in Jesus!

Is there a fog in your life that is keeping you from real happiness? Why not let the love of God, the strength of the Risen Christ, and the closeness of the Holy Spirit dry it up to expose the real message—trust in faith for you are not alone.

Confused, disappointed, etc., is only half the message; Christ will bring the other half, and this will completely change the meaning. Fear will turn to "I can," and hurt will turn to "I forgive."

Be careful, the evil one is probably preparing a fog for you right this very day.

* * * * *

First and foremost, faith to enter the Kingdom of God is childlike. Does anyone remember reading Hank Ketcham's comic strip, *Dennis the Menace*? The Wilsons are Dennis's next-door neighbors. In one cartoon episode, Mrs. Wilson tells Dennis that

Mr. Wilson was once just like him. Dennis then explains to a friend that once upon a time Mr. Wilson got dirty, had fights, stole cookies, and broke things, etc. just the way Dennis did.

To which the friend replied, "Gee, he sounds like a regular fella. I wonder when he went wrong."

Is it possible that's what Jesus might ask us? Where did you go wrong? What have you been aiming at? Personal ambition; personal power; manipulation of a loved one; prestige; personal ambition; your needs above all else? You are going the wrong way.

The Kingdom is this way. Jesus was trying to tell His disciples, "Fellows, you've got it all wrong—arguing about what you've done and who will get the chief seats in the Kingdom, you've missed the point. You're headed in the wrong direction. Unless you turn and become like children, you won't even get into the Kingdom."

Faith to enter the Kingdom is childlike because children have the capacity to trust. To a child, a state of dependence is a perfectly natural state.

* * * * *

On a warm summer morning, a preacher noticed that many in the congregation were drowsy. She paused her sermon and said, "Once I called at a farm and behold a most unusual sight I did see. I saw four little lambs, and each one had a long, five-foot, curved horn growing out of the middle of its back and . . ."

The clergywoman paused again and said, "How strange. Five minutes ago, I was preaching the truth, and most of you dozed. Now I tell you a whopper of a lie, and you're all ears!"

Maybe we take the gospel good news story for granted, and it no longer excites us. It's such an awesome story that includes our very salvation. How can we get excited again?

* * * * *

There are times when things kind of get mixed up, like the golden anniversary party thrown for an elderly couple. The husband was moved by the occasion and wanted to tell his wife just how he felt about her. She was very hard of hearing, however, and often misunderstood what he said. With many family members and friends gathered around, he toasted her. "My dear wife, after fifty years, I've found you tried and true!"

Everyone smiled approval, but the wife said, "Eh, what's that?"

He repeated louder, "After fifty years, I've found you tried and true!"

His wife shot back, "Well, let me tell you something—after fifty years, I'm tired of you too!"

PRAYER

Dear God of Power and Might, as I study and learn from the stories given to me in my Bible, I can see Your hand at work in Your people's lives. You come in small ways, as well as life-changing events. You come in the quietness of the moment, as well as the busyness of the day. Sometimes, Forgiving God, I do not recognize You because I was not expecting Your presence.

I profess to be a person of faith, yet I often feel I have to "go it alone," figure it out for myself. It must sadden You not to be included as a partner in my life's decisions, especially when I fall prey to satan's wily ways. You do not give me stress but rather the peace to know that this too shall pass.

Events can strengthen me under Your care, and yet I do not seek Your will. You do not give me worry but rather a quietness of spirit, knowing that whatever I might lose and might not have wanted to lose, You will show me how I have been misdirected and really didn't need something that was impeding my spiritual journey. And yet I prefer to battle satan alone.

In my heart, I know all I need on my spiritual journey is Your love and Your grace for all the earthly days I am given and then the extraordinary presence of Your heavenly home. And yet . . . help me, through the Holy Spirit, to learn not to spend so much energy on the perishable and material things of this world but rather to spend more time cultivating my relationship with You, inviting Your guidance, and worshiping You, not only on Sunday but in all aspects of my life.

Dear God, walk with me as I confront the dark places of my being as I face satan. Speak to me Your truth as I seek changes in my behavior. May I learn in love to treat others as I would have them treat me. Give me a right spirit that I may not shy from, but even seek out, the least, lost, and lonely. That I may be Your feet to go, Your hands to help, Your ears to hear their story, and Your mouth to proclaim the gospel good news story of hope and salvation.

And, dear God, let my steps be lighter as I cast off the harmful baggage of the past, the "shoulds and oughts" instilled in me by others, the controlling influence of hurtful behavior. Set me free, O God, to seek Your vision for my life and to soar with You as never before as I use my gifts and talents. Strengthen my desire to be all that I can be in Your name. Whatever my mission or vocation in life, I will involve You and live under the umbrella of Your grace, guidance, and love. These things I pray in the name of Jesus who taught the prayer saying, "Our Father . . ."

For the Christian, It Really Isn't a Choice

SERMONETTE

1 Corinthians 1:26-31

How old were you when you discovered that your parents weren't perfect? And isn't it interesting that they had to have a license to drive, fish, marry, among other things, but didn't need to have a license to have you! Everyone assumed they knew what to do.

And if they had character flaws, and you have children, are you passing on to them any of your parents' weaknesses that have become a part of your life? It seems that to be a successful father, son, mother, or daughter, there are times when situations dictate that guidance is needed. What set of values do you use and where did they come from?

Indeed, children don't come with a set of written instructions as to the way to develop their moral, ethical, and spiritual ways. But yet, as God's children, we *do* have a set of written instructions and values—the Bible. Did your parents share the stories in the Bible with you? Do you share them with your children? If you don't read and study the Bible, how do you know how to develop their spiritual life? After all, God is the source of love, wisdom, discernment, etc.

I would hold that many fathers have abdicated their biblical role as the spiritual head of the household. There is very little family prayer, grace over meals, and bedtime prayer. I'm not suggesting a dictator, but a spiritual head of the household who is concerned about spiritual development and who has respect and encouragement for all members of the family. One who is uplifting and supports all members of the family to blossom with their gifts and talents. What lesson is being taught when a mother and children attend Sunday school and worship and the father stays home?

Also, it's a part of raising children that parents are called upon to discipline certain behaviors. But how do you discern the boundaries of discipline unless you learn to pray over actions seeking wisdom and love? You can't always do it "like Mom and Dad did." Some of your quirks attest to that!

And as Christian parents, we are reminded that, as God's children, we may at times need to be disciplined also. Just as the Christian father is to discipline out of love, not anger or hurtful self-interest, God also disciplines out of love. Do you ever remember saying to a child, "Why didn't you ask me first before you did it?"

As the adult, do we go to God first or do we act on impulse, and, when it's not successful, try and have God "make it right"? Even when we consider running a proposed action by God, if we have an innate feeling that the answer will be no, we don't ask because we want to do it our way. In this circumstance, it appears better to ask for forgiveness than permission!

As a teenager, some of the neighborhood boys and I built a log fort in the back woods. A ladder had to be used to get to the top where the door into the fort was located. Did I mention we had a live stove for heat in this death trap?

My mother found out about it, she told the other mothers, and we boys spent time tearing down this beautiful edifice. We were asked why we didn't ask them first. The answer is simple—we knew they would say no, and we wanted our way!

It's a challenging responsibility being a Christian father or mother. It's important that we identify, with God's help through the Holy Spirit, our unhealthy baggage or unhealthy behavior that we travel with from family and friends. Prejudice in racial matters, hate, selfish behavior, etc. In prayer, make changes—don't pass it on! Seek guidance in prayer and Scripture reading from your heavenly Father. Discipline with love and respect—talk it over with God first, be a Christian spiritual leader. And when you feel you have a request for God but are unsure whether or not to pray over it, that's a sure sign you need to pray over it!

Your way might be quicker but will probably turn out with more problems. So here's the question—God's way or your way? When they aren't the same, which path were you taught to take and do you still take it?

ILLUSTRATIONS

As we show special recognition to the mothers of the church, we want to talk about something very special. Maybe we can start to get a glimpse of it today in the story of a lady who knocked at her neighbor's door.

Gene, a six-year-old, appeared. "Hello, Gene, are you there all alone?" the old lady said with concern.

"Yes," said the youngster sadly. "My mother is in the hospital, and me and daddy and my two sisters and two brothers and two uncles are here all alone!"

Maybe we can get another glimpse in the story of the lady who, after watching a mother with her four grown sons and daughters, commented, "I'd give thirty years of my life to have four children like yours."

The mother answered, "Believe me, that's about what it took!"

Or maybe we can find something in the story of Tony Pena, a catcher for the Boston Red Sox. Tony grew up in the Dominican Republic where life wasn't very easy. Tony says that the person who had the greatest influence on his life was his mother. It's the dream of many boys in the Dominican Republic to play baseball in the United States. Knowing of his love for the game, each day when school was out, his mother took him to the nearby pasture. She stood on a rough dirt patch that served as the pitcher's mound and worked with him hour after hour.

Mothers are very special, and on Father's Day, we will say the same about fathers. But most special of all are Christian mothers and fathers. Those mothers and fathers who take it upon themselves to be Christian examples for their children. When the Apostle Paul wrote, "Children, obey your parents," he was assuming the reader in the church to which he was writing was Christian.

Mothers are very special and they also have a very special task—to let their children and those around them see Christ in action. As we honor mothers, let us lift them up as Christian leaders in the family.

* * * * *

Sam remembers how, as a young child, he got so excited when his parents told him the family was going to visit his favorite aunt and uncle. This couple was loved by Sam for two reasons: Aunt Mae always had plenty of fresh chocolate cookies, and Uncle Jimmy would do a magic trick by finding a quarter behind each of Sam's ears. Uncle Jimmy was very friendly and fun to be around, but the best part was Sam got to keep the quarter from behind each ear.

At the age of ten, Sam was conspiring as to how he might get two more quarters from behind his elbows. So, when his father announced a visit to Uncle Jimmy and Aunt Mae on Monday of the next week, he was very happy. That would give him several days to practice his approach to receiving more quarters. He thought enthusiastically about the gift of meeting Uncle Jimmy and getting free quarters.

As Sam grew older, many times he wondered why he felt uneasy over meeting Jesus and receiving the free gift of salvation. Could we have some apprehension that Christ will ask, "What did you do during your life's journey on earth to further my Kingdom?"

Take a moment now—what will your answer be?

* * * * *

As we celebrate with fathers on Father's Day, we realize that fathers sometimes get a bum rap. For instance, one comic claimed that the people of ancient Israel would not have wandered for forty years in the wilderness if Moses had only stopped to ask for directions. But why would he? He was a man!

We have a gene that predestines us to believe, "I can do it. Trust me. It might take me two hours as opposed to fifteen minutes if I stopped at the gas station and asked for directions, but I can do this—I can figure it out on my own!"

And of course, storytellers show fathers no mercy. The story is told of a family who had three small children who were determined to have a puppy. Mother protested because she knew somehow she would end up caring for the pup. The children solemnly promised they would take care of it if only she would let them have a puppy. Finally, she relented and they brought their little puppy home and named him Danny.

They cared for him diligently—for a while. Time passed and Mom found herself responsible for the dog. She became resolved to find a new home for Danny. She was quite surprised at the children's reaction.

Said one child, "We'll miss him."

One child said, "If he didn't eat so much and wouldn't be so messy, could he stay?"

Mom held her ground and told the children, "It's time to take Danny to a new home."

With one voice and tearful outrage the children screamed all together, "Danny, we thought you said Daddy!!"

Fathers get no respect, no respect at all.

* * * * *

On this Father's Day, we recognize one of the attributes of being a father is leadership. This is exemplified by the father who won a toy in a magazine subscription promotion. Being the leader of the household, he called his three children together to see who would receive this prize. And to set the ground rules for awarding the prize, he asked, "Who is the most obedient?"

Then he asked, "Who never talks back to Mother?"

And finally, "Who does everything mother says?"

Three small voices answered in unison, "If those are the rules, then you get to keep the toy, Daddy!"

* * * * *

A newspaper editor once asked his daughter to write a feature article, a story about David Livingstone, the great missionary. But this editor had left his religion behind him long ago. He wanted a story of the man Livingstone, the do-gooder, the humanitarian, but he didn't want it colored by all that missionary stuff. "Leave his Christianity out of it," he told his daughter. "Don't mention his religion!"

And she set off to research her assignment, and she came back almost at once. "It's impossible," she said. "It can't be done! The man and his faith are one and the same thing! You can't speak of Livingstone without speaking of his Christ."

Would a part of our eulogy be, "In him/her we saw Jesus Christ?"

PRAYER

Most trustworthy God, sometimes I feel there is too much going on. I have opportunities to do many things. Often, circumstances lead me down a certain path, or a sense of obligation drains my energy. Aspects of the world seem so inviting, and I make a conscious decision to try and do as much as I can in my quest for happiness. I seem to have within me a feeling that all is well the busier I am. Or that peace can only be found in withdrawal as life is just too hard and complicated. I sometimes have a sense of uneasiness as the world seems to be falling apart. And yet You are still God. You are still on the throne for eternity. You still call me through the Holy Spirit to Your way as witnessed in the life of Jesus.

Satan still tries to confuse me in that the world says, "Get all you can," but Your Word in Scripture says, "Give all you can."

In many ways, the world teaches that we need to be concerned about only taking care of ourselves. Your Word directs us to help in the care of others whose circumstances have given them a hard earthly journey. The world lets me know I should love those who think, act, and look like me. Although I don't have to love all behavior, I often find it is difficult to love the person as one of Your created children, as I am also.

Dear God of wisdom and love, steer me onto the path of seeking soul-satisfying joy and not just the fleeting times of happiness. Happiness is so dependent on my circumstances. Give me an inner desire to seek lasting joy which comes from my relationship with You through the Holy Spirit and the Living Jesus the Christ. May I come to truly know that as I pass through my earthly journey, true peace, true joy, true hope, true love—these things I seek—are made possible only through a lasting relationship of faith and trust in You.

Dear God, I ask for Your special attention to those I lift up to You silently from my heart.

I continue to pray for your guidance to world leaders that their hearts will be moved to world peace. These I pray in the name of Jesus who taught the prayer saying, "Our Father . . ."

Why Not Accept It?

SERMONETTE

2 Corinthians 3:17-18

We have many references in the Bible where Jesus said this, or that, or the other. Did you ever wonder who was recording these utterances verbatim? Is each word attributed to Him exactly the word He used? At the time of Jesus, people didn't carry notebooks and pencils, cellphones, and tape recorders, and there was no secretary to follow Jesus to take dictation.

The first four gospel writers of the New Testament (Matthew, Mark, Luke, and John) didn't put the words on paper until at least fifty years after the death of Jesus. So, what faith can we have that Jesus was accurately quoted every time we read, "Jesus said"?

It's the very absence of the above devices that gives us confidence that He is quoted correctly. People in Jesus's day were experts at repeating accurately what they heard and saw. The story you heard about Jesus in Galilee would be identical to the version you heard in Capernaum. The message Jesus was giving was always understood the same, wherever the message was given.

There were times the religious leaders tried to trip Him up and get different answers, like the time they asked Him if they should pay taxes. A yes or a no would get Him in trouble. You might remember Jesus asked to see a coin and then asked, "Whose picture is on it?"

They replied, "Caesar's."

"Then return to Caesar what is his, and to God what is His."

And when Jesus told the Apostles He was going to leave them, they wanted real answers. "What is going to happen to us?"

And in all accounts, the answer is the same. Jesus reassured them by conveying that He would ask the Father to send the Counselor, the Spirit of Truth, the Comforter, the Holy Spirit, to be with them forever. His words in John 14:17 were, "This Holy Spirit will live with you and will be in you."

Although the word "trinity" is not found in the Bible, we see it here as God, God in Jesus, and God as Holy Spirit. Only one God, but three aspects of God's nature. For a good account of the sending of the Holy Spirit following the death of Jesus, read Acts 2:1-10 concerning the day of Pentecost.

But the Holy Spirit didn't come just for the Apostles. It's for everyone who believes in the gospel good news story! Jesus knew the Apostles would have an empty feeling and, left to their own ways, would stand a good chance of not holding together against satan. They needed a powerful Guide, a personal Presence found in them always pointing them to God, strength, and direction.

Have you ever felt alone? Please don't. Please be assured that you are not! In your baptism where you became a part of God's family, the Holy Spirit came to reside within your very being. We are Spirit-filled with a force that is a part of God's will, and when we follow the Spirit (especially in bad times), it will lead to a peace that passes all human understanding. An acceptance of this basic biblical truth can be life-changing. We come to know and feel peace in the fruits of the Holy Spirit: love, joy, patience, kindness, goodness, faithfulness, gentleness, and self-control.

We are also confident in the position that when satan tries to ruin our day, we can say, "Get away from me for I am Spirit-led in Jesus the Risen Savior under the umbrella of God's love."

Jesus told us he was going to prepare a place for us, and that he would have the Comforter and Advocate sent to us by the Father.

He said, "Receive the Holy Spirit" (John 20:22). Jesus does not lie. You have not been alone; you travel on your earthly journey with the Spirit of God within you. You already have what it takes to cure that lonely feeling. Why not accept it and use it?

ILLUSTRATIONS

The story is told of Admiral Byrd, the famous explorer, who once found himself about one hundred yards away from the safety of his South Pole hut when a sudden blizzard hit.

The temperature was several degrees below zero, and the snow was blinding. There were no landmarks in the white expanse of snow and ice-covered sea that would help him get his bearings. Yet he knew that if he didn't find the warmth and safety of his hut, he would freeze to death in a matter of minutes.

Admiral Byrd couldn't see his hut or anything else in that freezing blizzard that would guide him to safety. He also knew that if he struck out blindly, without a central reference point for a sense of direction, he would become hopelessly lost. Refusing to panic, the Admiral assessed the situation. In his hand was a ten-foot pole that he carried with him to probe for holes in the ice as he walked. He stuck the pole in the snow and tied his brightly colored scarf to it. Then he began looking for the hut, keeping the pole in sight as a reference point, knowing that he could always return if necessary.

He struck out first in one direction, then in another, always keeping the pole and scarf in sight. Three times he came back to his point of reference; on the fourth try, he found the hut. His life was saved because he maintained a point of reference.

The Bible is the point of reference for the Christian. We can't listen to Christ or the apostles preach, but we can read their testimony. What point of reference do you use in your life? Will it benefit you? Will it fatten your bank account? Will it give you power and prestige? These things don't require Bible reading.

But for the one trying to find God, through Jesus and the Holy Spirit, the reference point needs to be the Word to receive the true Light. As you consider the time you spend reading the Bible, what reference can you draw about your reference point in life?

* * * * *

The time of judgment, how will it play out?

Only moments after prying open a window and stepping into a dark bedroom, a burglar came face to face with a big, vicious-looking Doberman Pinscher. The burglar froze in his tracks. Once his eyes adjusted to the dark, he noticed a parrot was sitting on the back of the dog, and the parrot squawked, "You're gonna get caught."

Without any sudden or jerky movements, the burglar then cleaned the valuable items from the top of the dresser. The dog glared. The parrot said, "You're gonna get caught."

The burglar quietly left the room, walked down the hallway, entered another room. The dog followed his every movement in the hall and the next room. The parrot squawked, "You're gonna get caught."

From room to room, the dog paced right behind the burglar while the parrot annoyingly shouted, "You're gonna get caught." At last, the burglar finished stealing the jewelry and the cash. Every move by every muscle was scrutinized by the big Doberman. The parrot said, "You're gonna get caught."

Exasperated, the burglar finally bent over and picked up a shoe. He threw it at the bird and said, "You dumb parrot! Can't you say anything else?"

The parrot fluttered away to avoid the shoe but this time said, "Sure can. Sic 'em, boy!"

For that man, the great burglar day of judgment was at hand.

* * * * *

There's a silly story aimed at fictitious astronauts, but it could be aimed at many of us. It seems that three astronauts were selected to participate in a two-year mission in space. At a prelaunch briefing, the astronauts were told that they could take anything with them as long as it didn't weigh more than 122 pounds. Said the first astronaut, "My wife weighs one hundred and twenty-two pounds, I'll take her."

The officials said that was fine. "I've always wanted to learn Greek," the second astronaut said. "I'd like one hundred and twenty-two pounds of books to teach myself the language."

His request was also approved. "We'll be gone so long," the third astronaut said, "that I want to take one hundred and twenty-two pounds of the best cigars with me." His request was okayed also.

Two years later, they all returned to earth. The first astronaut stepped out of the spaceship holding an infant in each arm. There was a roar of approval from the crowd. The second stepped out and spoke to the crowd in flawless Greek. Again, there was a roar of approval. Then the third astronaut stepped out. His mouth was turned down and his teeth were clenched on a well-chewed and soggy cigar. He stepped up to the microphone and said nervously, "Please, please, does anyone have a match!"

How often do we find ourselves in an unpleasant situation because we didn't plan and are not adequately prepared? While the cigars are on the moon, the matches are still on earth.

Some time back, in a real, true-life situation, one of the astronauts was asked before a moon mission, "What's the most dangerous part of the flight?"

He answered, "The part we don't prepare for."

Most of the time, preparation is so important. The motto of the Boy Scouts is, "Be Prepared." It's a great motto for this life and in conjunction with the next life. Many times, we hear, "When you die, you take nothing with you."

That's simply not true. You take your relationship with Jesus the Christ with you. That ultimately determines your final home. How is your preparation coming along?

* * * * *

When was the last time you experienced an embarrassing moment, and what was the occasion? A man was in a grocery store and noticed the back of his neighbor, who was walking down the aisle in front of him. The man thought he would play a prank on his neighbor, so he sneaked up behind him and in a loud voice said, "I saw you put that jar of peanut butter under your coat. Put it back on the shelf!"

The neighbor turned around abruptly, except it wasn't the neighbor.

We all can come up with our embarrassing moments, most involving a mistake. There is one mistake many are making which, one day, will be frightening and embarrassing. One day, the trumpet will sound, and everyone will be ushered into God's presence with only their relationship to Jesus going with them from their earthly home. No time to prepare further. In a twinkling of an eye, we will be in God's presence to give an account. Is it time to do some planning or just put it off until another day? Are you sure you will get that day?

* * * * *

In March of 1843, George Frederick Handel's *Messiah* and *Hallelujah Chorus* was heard for the first time in London. The success and appreciation accorded to the work—considered by many to be the greatest of all musical works—was instantaneous. While it has been nearly two centuries since this great oratorio was first written, it still occupies a place in the program of nearly every great music festival around the world. It has doubtless been heard by larger audiences and a greater number of people than any other sacred music ever composed.

Handel loved Bible stories. He remembered that Jesus led His disciples out of the city and along the road toward Bethany, and there, while they were gazing steadfastly at Him, He disappeared in a cloud from their sight. In his imagination, Handel tried to picture what was happening behind that cloud. And in his musical story, the angel's *Hallelujah Chorus*, he tells us what he thinks happened.

Handel believed that God sent His angels to meet Jesus and to bring Him with songs of rejoicing into the heavenly home. He thought that other angels stayed by the Gates of heaven to greet Jesus as He arrived. And he felt that these angels were so happy, they sang songs of joy while they waited. Handel remembered a poetic psalm which he thought expressed the words the angels must have been singing. For in Psalm 24:7, we find, "Lift up your heads, you gates; be so lifted up, you ancient doors, that the King of Glory may come in."

Handel imagined the angels at the gates answered, "Who is this King of Glory?"

And the angels accompanying Jesus replied, "The Lord, strong and mighty." Then the angels who kept the heavenly entrance opened wide the gates, and Jesus, the King of Glory, passed through them into His father's house.

The last words of the *Hallelujah Chorus* are, "And He shall reign forever and ever. King of Kings and Lord of Lords, Hallelujah, Hallelujah, Hallelujah, Hallelujah."

When you hear the mighty swell of this triumphant climax of the angel chorus, you don't wonder that Queen Victoria, when first she heard Handel's *Messiah*, laid aside her crown and stood with her husband in recognition that the King of kings, who is above all and who must reign supreme in every life, triumphs. At Easter time and especially on Ascension Sunday, when we remember the joyous return of Jesus to His heavenly home, we should keep ringing in our ears and our hearts the angels' *Hallelujah Chorus*.

Let us remember to live as Christ would have us live as we continue to tell the story of His love to others everywhere. "I go to prepare a place for you." Just think about what that means!

PRAYER

Dear Omnipotent God, as You are the very force of creation and the Provider and Sustainer of all that is good, I humbly witness before You my proclamation of glory and praise to Your ever presence.

I'm reminded of how things in my life can change, and I have to find different responses rather than my planned behavior. In this process, my journey is made even more peaceful by knowing You are the same today as yesterday and will be the same tomorrow. Your love and ever-presence in the Holy Spirit can be my foundation of peace in all matters. For I find hope in my very being, knowing that this earthly home is not my final resting place. That the presence of Your heavenly home can be mine for repentance and acceptance of Jesus as Lord and Savior of my life.

Now, as I come to a place in my faith, merciful God, where I recognize my mortality. I also reflect on how I allow my behavior to be less than pleasing to You. Often my actions reflect my self-interest and the pursuit of false gods. I pray for Your forgiveness and may I, in strength and conviction, be led to give up ways and things which lessen my stature as Your worthwhile child and brother (or sister) of Christ. Enliven me to seek Your ways with greater effort that hope, peace, joy, and love may be mine now and eternally.

Dear compassionate God, I not only lift myself up to You but also family and friends, especially those who do not know You or whose faith is tested by sickness or other adversities. May they be assured of Your peaceful love now and that placing their soul in Your hands through Jesus allows them a home for eternity. Let their peace, as well as mine, be bound up in faith, trust, and love for You as our God of yesterday, today, and tomorrow.

I continue to pray that Your strength, power, and direction be felt by those in leadership positions throughout all countries. These things I ask in the precious name of Jesus who taught the prayer saying, "Our Father . . ."

What Road Are You On?

SERMONETTE

Philippians 4:4-9

Probably the most well-known personality in the New Testament besides Jesus was the Apostle Paul (known first as Saul). Saul was traveling to Damascus to persecute the Christians living there. On the road, a light from heaven flashed around him. He fell to the ground and heard a voice say, "Saul, Saul, why do you persecute me?"

Saul asked, "Who are you, Lord?"

"I am Jesus whom you are persecuting," He replied.

When Saul opened his eyes, he could see nothing, so those traveling led him to the city. For the rest of the story see Acts 9:9-19.

I expect your encounter with Jesus was not this dramatic. Paul's experience with Jesus allowed him to claim to be the thirteenth Apostle (some disagreed with him as the original twelve were chosen by Jesus while He was in human form, and we call them Apostles as they were specially commissioned by Christ).

We are all "disciples" or "followers" of Christ but the twelve and Paul were all given special assignments. Paul changed completely, and instead of persecuting he began to preach the gospel good news story of Jesus the Christ. From his conversion, he always had a thankful heart for his new life. He preached that we should be thankful *in* all things. He did not preach that we should be thankful *for* all things.

You don't have to be thankful *for* the dead battery in your car, but you need to be thankful that *in* this, the presence of God through the Holy Spirit will give you wisdom, strength, patience, and understanding to solve the problem. You might even consider being thankful that you even have a car! One important thing about Paul—no matter what his situation, he prayed and gave thanks that the Spirit of God was with him. Paul acted with confidence and strength and helped show us that God did not give disciples, including us, a spirit of timidity and fear. You have to understand that your words, thoughts, and actions testify to your level of faith. The words of Paul are "Do not be ashamed to testify about Jesus."

But this means you have to get to know Jesus personally; don't know *about* Jesus, for even the devil knows that! We need to remember these points: Jesus lived as the presence of God in human form (incarnate); Jesus was crucified and bore with Him our sins so that by calling Him Lord and Savior, we may be redeemed (made right with God); and with God's power, Jesus arose from the grave, giving rise to our hopeful excitement of our resurrection to the heavenly realm.

In Christ, (1) Believe and act like you are saved, (2) Have a thankful heart *in* all things, (3) Recognize the Holy Spirit within you, (4) Don't be timid in your faith, (5) Last, but certainly not least, be aware of any bargaining and compromise with sin. When you hear, "It won't hurt to do it just one time," know that is a slippery slope and one of satan's best ploys.

Be thankful that, *IN* all things, you have the option to follow Jesus the Christ. Sounds like a good spiritual road to follow. What do you think and feel about that?

ILLUSTRATIONS

THE BIKE RIDE

At first, I saw God as my observer, my judge keeping track of what I did. I recognized God's existence but really didn't know God. But later, when I met Christ as my Lord and Savior, it seemed as though life was rather like a bike ride, but it was a tandem bike, and I noticed Christ was in the back helping me pedal.

I don't know just when it happened that He suggested we change places, and life has not been the same since. Christ makes things and life exciting.

When I had control, I knew the way. It was rather boring, but predictable . . . it was the shortest distance between two points. But when He took the lead, He delightfully took long cuts, up mountains and through rocky places at a fast speed. It was all I could do to hold on! Even though it looked like madness, He said, "Pedal."

I was worried and anxious and asked, "Where are you taking me?" He laughed and didn't answer, and I started to trust and have faith. I forgot my boring life and entered the adventure.

And when I said, "I'm scared," He'd lean back and touch my hand.

He took me to people with gifts that I needed, gifts of healing, acceptance, and joy. They gave me their gifts to take on my journey, my Lord's and mine, and we were off again. He said, "Give the gifts away; they're extra baggage, too much weight."

So I gave to people we met, and I found that in giving I received, and still our burden was light. I did not trust Him at first, in control of my life. I thought He would wreck it, but He knows bike secrets, knows how to make it bend to take sharp corners, jump to clear high rocks, fly to shorten scary passages.

I'm learning to shut up and pedal in the strangest places, and I'm beginning to enjoy the view and the cool breeze on my face as never before, with my delightful constant companion, Jesus the Christ. And when I feel like I just can't do it anymore, He just smiles and says, "Pedal."

* * * * *

William Volker, the inventor of the roll-up window shade, gave away enormous amounts of money. While still a

50

comparatively young man, he was worth several millions of dollars. He gave away so much money that his friends thought he had taken leave of his senses. They were concerned about the money he was "shoveling out." He replied, "Yes, I have been shoveling it out, but God has been shoveling more of it right back to me, and God has a bigger shovel!"

Jesus preached many times on the motivation for giving. We are to look at how God has blessed us, and in prayer, the amount is set. Giving is never tied to the church receipts. Whether the church is in the red or black, it's a personal arrangement between you and God, taking into consideration how you have been blessed. Every church has enough money, however, sometimes it's in the pockets of the members.

* * * * *

"What's around the corner?" asked a curious little child as she sat with her father in the doctor's waiting room. At the end of the room, there was a fascinating hall that disappeared around a corner. Maybe beyond her view was a candy machine or a playroom or toys around that corner. She eased out of her seat as if drawn to explore the alluring unknown around the corner.

"Or maybe around the corner," her father ominously predicted, "is the examination room where you will get your shot!"

The little girl quickly jumped securely into her chair and held on for dear life. In one unforeseeable moment of surprise in that doctor's waiting room, out of the mystery and shadows around that fascinating corner, came the doctor herself. She was well-loved and trusted by the little girl who eased forward in her chair again. This time she reached out her hand. She was ready and willing to go into the unknown because she knew who would go with her around the corner. And knowing who will be with you as you go around the corner every time is far more important than knowing what is around the corner.

"I know not what the future hath of marvel or surprise. Assured alone that life and death His mercy underlies. I know not where His islands lift their palms in air; I only know that I cannot drift beyond His love and care."

This unknown author affirmed that God is the *Who* in our future. Thus, by faith, we dare to go with God into the mysteries of the unknown. Isn't it comforting to know that you aren't alone, ever?

* * * * *

We are Christians; we walk with Christ. Can you tell what that has meant to you in your life?

An atheist was seated beside a man on a bus, and during their conversation, the man allowed that he was a member of a Christian church. "Well," said the atheist, "I guess you still eat three meals a day."

"Yes, I do," said the Christian.

"And I suppose you work at least forty hours a week and go to sleep at night."

"Why, yes I do," said the Christian.

"And I suppose this week you have had some leisure time, spent some with your family or friends."

"Why, yes," said the humble Christian.

"Well," said the atheist, "you see, this week I did each of these things also. How was your life different from mine this week? You believe in Jesus as your Christ—I don't. How was your life lived any different from mine this week?"

Now, I want to ask you to imagine yourself seated beside the atheist and you have just been asked, "You believe in Jesus as your Christ—I don't. How has your life been lived any different from mine this past week?"

What would your answer be? I believe your answer is part of your faith story. A personal walk with Jesus will give one answer but just knowing about Jesus won't be much above the position of the atheist. Do you have a good answer?

* * * * *

Remember Gracie Allen who played the scatterbrained wife in a comedy team with her husband, George Burns? (If you do, you are not a youngster by any means.) In the routine, Gracie called in a repairman to fix her electric clock. The repairman fiddled with it for a while and then told her, "There's nothing wrong with the clock; you just have to have it plugged in."

Gracie replied, "I don't want to waste electricity, so I only plug it in when I want to know what time it is."

I believe that's a good description of many of us. We save our religion for a rainy day. We go about unplugged and wonder why our lives are so devoid of power. That's sad. Christian faith is not something to be plugged in when it's convenient. The Christian faith is to be lived daily.

The Apostle Paul writes in Scripture that nothing can separate us from God, and he lists many things which are not able to separate us. But I believe there is one thing which can separate us—we can do it. We can let our light become dim. Why not decide today to get plugged in?

PRAYER

Ever-present God of hope and love, each and every day of my life I must make decisions. The very existence of life brings challenges, surprises, setbacks, and joys, and at the end of the day, many things have been decided. Some are life-changing, many are minor, some affect others, some affect only my well-being. Throughout the day, I must also decide how often I will bring you into the complex or routine events which I face.

I'm tempted to believe that my strength is sufficient, and I am able to understand fully what is best for me. Many times I find, through the sinister force of temptation and dishonesty, I have allowed myself to engage life in behavior that is not Christlike, even selfish behavior without regard for others or my spiritual values. Many times I want to receive Your blessings, but I want to receive them *my* way.

Dear God, give me the spiritual insight to see that when I close my heart and mind to Your direction, I forfeit beautiful, uplifting experiences. Forgive me, I pray, for those times I have proceeded alone. Let Your Holy Spirit direct me in the ways I can be bold in service to You. Give me the desire to fully live and use in Your service the gifts and talents I have been given.

Hear my petition, loving God, for those I place before You in my heart. Let those named and those around them find peace in increased faith and trust as they await Your movement in their lives. What we see as challenges, You use as opportunities for increased closeness with You. I continue to ask that Your Spirit will lead people away from differences to similarities, from terror and bondage to freedom and openness. Uphold those who strive for peace. These I ask in the name of our Lord and Savior, Jesus the Christ who taught the prayer, saying, "Our Father . . ."

What Would It Take?

SERMONETTE

Hebrews 12:1-3

The Christian year is divided into sections. You have Advent (four Sundays before Christmas proclaiming the coming), Christmas (birth story), Epiphany (the "aha" time when we really see who Jesus is), Lent (the forty weekdays of penitence and giving up bad behavior), Easter (the resurrection of Jesus), and Pentecost (when the Holy Spirit was received).

The seasons best known are Christmas and Easter. People who attend only these two days a year are referred to as "C and E" people. Christmas begins the story of Jesus's life, and Easter tells us there is more than just death. After His resurrection, Jesus appeared to over five hundred people we are aware of. Many people didn't recognize Him; could be because of their sorrow or His appearance was different. They were also afraid and disappointed. They, especially the Apostles, had given up so much.

After Jesus's death, when the two Marys went to the tomb, they took supplies to take care of the body. They didn't expect to see an empty tomb. When they told the Apostles, they were hesitant to believe Jesus wasn't still dead. In fact, Thomas said, "Unless I see the nail marks in his hands and put my finger where the nails were, and put my hand into his side, I will not believe" (John 20:24).

Lack of evidence had tripped up their faith. Have you ever felt Jesus let you down? Life seemed at a crossroads, and Jesus didn't make the path smooth. Maybe you felt let down because you were looking for the wrong thing!

Many times, we pray the answer. "O Lord, if you would just do . . ." instead of seeking the answer, "O Lord, send me the wisdom to discern and act upon Your desire."

Jesus appeared to the disciples and gave Thomas the opportunity to touch Him, but Thomas was overwhelmed and only said, "My Lord and my God" (John 20:28).

What do you need to fully accept Him as Lord and Savior of your very soul and invite Him into your being? Jesus said, "Because you have seen me, you have believed; blessed are those who have not seen and yet have believed" (John 20:29).

What do you need to accept the gospel good news stories of Jesus to believe? We have to remember we travel spiritually by faith, not relying on facts. We don't prove it; we believe it, and then it becomes real to us. Does Jesus have to appear physically to you for you to follow Him? In the presence of only select facts, what does it take for you to come from *maybe* to *in faith I am sure*?

Our seasons tell us (1) Jesus is the Christ (God incarnate, God in human form), (2) He lived, preached, and healed, (3) He suffered and took our sins upon Himself, (4) God reached into the tomb and took Jesus to Himself, (5) Because Jesus defeated death and was resurrected, we can be also by accepting Christ, and (6) The resurrected Jesus had God send the Holy Spirit to us to comfort and counsel.

With all that the five seasons tell about the joy of belief, do you still have to put your finger in His side?

ILLUSTRATIONS

There was a make-believe workshop where all the tools began to argue over who was most important. The first to speak was Mr. Tape Measure, who felt he certainly deserved the honor, for without him there would be no measurements to guide the work. With a murmur, one of the other tools complained that Mr. Tape Measure always judged others while assuming he always was right.

Mr. Hammer was next, and he suggested that he had more power than the others combined and, without him, not a single nail could be driven. Someone commented that all his banging was disruptive to the work of the others.

Mr. Screw thought he deserved the honor because when he attached two things together, they stayed together. A low voice was heard to say that the only way Mr. Screw got any work done was to have someone constantly turn him around.

Other tools made their pitch and a heated discussion ensued. But, all became quiet when Jesus arrived. He began to lay out all the materials needed to make a beautiful wooden container to hold the synagogue papers. He used practically every tool in the shop and, as he left the shop at the close of the day, he took with him the beautiful gift for the synagogue.

When all was quiet Mr. Hammer observed, under the direction of the carpenter, they all had worked well together. Under His leadership, they had worked together with a single purpose.

As you look at your situation, many aspects have to work together for you to attain a life of peace. There are interactions between mind, emotions, physical needs, and faith needs. All are important and when we, on our own, attempt to keep that peace, often the result is confusion. When Jesus Christ sits on the throne of our very being, we will find that the aspects of our lives really do work quite well together. What is to keep you from giving it a try?

* * * * *

A little girl had a cut near her eye. Her sister quickly took her to see the doctor. The cut was not serious but the location of the injury made it important that it be fixed properly. The doctor decided a couple of stitches were needed, but he didn't want to give the child an anesthetic. He explained to her that the procedure would have some pain and asked her if she could stand it. The little girl replied that she could if her sister would hold her hand. The sister then took her in her lap, slipped her arm around her sister, and held tight.

The doctor did his work, and the little girl never flinched. The sister could not possibly have eased the pain from the process but the girl needed to not be alone.

What a wonderful awareness for us to know that we are never alone. God's Spirit is over and within us. If you see me and you think I am talking to myself, I'm not talking to myself!!

* * * * *

We hear about the judgment day, and our Scriptures which have served us for two thousand years tell us there will be such an event and, further, that on that day, there will be a lot of surprises.

A man was seated on his living room floor involved with a book he was reading when his four-year-old daughter came up to him wanting attention. Holding a tube of what appeared to be flavored Chap Stick in her hand, she asked, "Want some?"

"Of course," he replied. Promptly, he carefully spread the soft lip balm on his lips while reading the book. It was an extremely sour Chap Stick but it felt good on his lips, so at her urging, he put another generous layer on his lips just as the girl's mother came calling through the house.

"Kortney, what did you do with my glue stick?"

SURPRISE. That's the sort of picture of the last day that Jesus gives to us; people are surprised. In the parable in Matthew 25:31-46, the sheep don't understand what they have done to experience being taken up to Jesus, and the goats don't understand why they're being guided toward the eternal fire. It seems to be the helpers versus the hoarders. The selfish versus the givers. What surprise is waiting for you?

* * * * *

The joy of God is so great when one of His children who is lost turns to Him and is brought back into the fold. How many times? Depends on how many times they are lost.

A certain man was gloriously converted one night during a revival service. He began sharing the story of his conversion in churches throughout the area. During one of these sharing sessions, someone suggested writing down the story of his conversion to prevent it from being lost. And so he did. Years later someone asked him about his conversion experience. "Well," he replied, "I have forgotten much of the details but I did write it down."

He turned to his granddaughter and said, "Honey, please go to my desk and bring the story of my conversion."

She returned with several sheets of yellowed, tattered paper just full of holes and said, "Grandpa, I hate to tell you this, but the roaches and silverfish have gotten into your conversion experience."

As hard as we try, there are times when things less desirable get into our conversion experience. There are times when our pride or desires, fanned by the sultry voice of the evil one, leads us to do something not pleasing to God—to wander—and, for a time, to be lost from God's purpose. The time we gave our life to Jesus the Christ should always be memorable and vivid within us. This assumes that the conversion experience was real and lead to a personal walk with Jesus. Is your conversion experience still alive within you? If not, I wonder why not.

* * * * *

A woman had a full medical examination. The doctor took his prescription pad and wrote, "Take this green pill in the morning with a full glass of water. Take the blue pill at lunch with a full glass of water, and take the red pill before going to bed with a full glass of water."

"Exactly what is wrong with me? What's my problem, Doctor?" she asked.

"You aren't getting enough water," he replied.

What do you reckon Jesus would prescribe when we aren't getting enough spiritual growth?

PRAYER

Ever-patient God, it's difficult sometimes for me to admit that I need You. I am so set on doing things myself, trusting my judgment alone which causes me to miss the subtleties and the manipulations of my ever-present enemy who delights and profits from my self-induced estrangement from You. I put my peace and joy at risk when I fall prey to satan's deceptions. With a humble heart, I seek Your forgiveness this day.

Let the truth of Your love burn so brightly within me that it will become my need to place matters before You and allow Your Holy Spirit to deflect satan's arrows. May the Holy Spirit lead me into an even deeper relationship with You through Jesus the Christ. You cared so much that I would take my place in Your heavenly home, that You came in the form of Jesus, to not only show me the pattern for my life, but You also suffered on the cross to bear my sins and spiritual shortcomings. Because of such love, He gave His life as a gift to me in order that His resurrection will allow me, as a believer in His name, to enjoy eternal life.

Allow me to see ever more clearly how my earthly journey can be more peaceful and my heavenly reception be more joyous when I allow You, the presence of Jesus, and the support of the Holy Spirit to become a vital, living, inseparable part of my life. As Jesus opened the minds of disciples, open my mind to the beauty of the gospel good news story of salvation, the saving of my very soul through Your grace, and my acceptance of Jesus, the Risen Savior, as Lord.

And, dear God, may I be ever mindful of the opportunities You give me to uplift those who are a part of or will become a part of my life. As You are generous, let the Holy Spirit lead me to be generous also. I pray that You will look with even more compassion on all those who have lost their health. Strengthen them in faith and recovery as You provide. To caregivers, grant patient understanding and a love that perseveres.

I continue to pray that the hatred found in the hearts of various world leaders will be replaced by Your divine presence. These things I ask in the precious name of Jesus who taught the prayer saying, "Our Father . . ."

Why Not Pick a Day?

SERMONETTE

John 3:1-21

Some events in life are more meaningful than others. You don't remember your physical birth (the moment you came from darkness to the light of the delivery room), but your birthday is a very important event. There is another event that has hopefully happened, and you might not remember just when or how it happened. For this. we use the term "born again."

In the New Testament Book of John, chapter three, Nicodemus, a very prominent Jew, basically asked Jesus, "How can I be saved?"

Jesus's answer surprised him, "You must be born again."

"How?" asked Nicodemus. "Do I have to go back into my mother's womb?"

Being born again is allowing the "old self" to die and then putting on the "new self" (Christ-centered). It's believing fully that Jesus is the Christ, the Messiah, and the Anointed One, and you relinquish your old sinful self. Does this mean you will never sin again and have become perfect? No—but when you are born again, you now try in all things to follow the light of Christ.

We understand, upon accepting Christ through God's grace, we have a way for salvation. One can be born again by using the sinner's prayer. "Lord, I am a sinner. I repent of my sins and ask for forgiveness. I accept Jesus the Christ as Lord and Savior of my life."

Once you make this heartfelt proclamation, your life will never be the same! You will view life and your actions from a totally different perspective. Although your journey to come to Christ might have been over time, why not reflect upon your journey and designate a day to celebrate as your spiritual birthday? A day when you came to fully realize your decision might not change the world but it will certainly make a world of difference to you! You will come alive in a different way.

You will also be enabled by the Holy Spirit to gain victory over the sinful patterns of life which satan presents to you. You will begin to see more fully that things of this world are only ships passing in the night, not to be confused with our path to eternity. We will trade gloom for glory, self for service, and gossip for the gospel good news story of Jesus.

Each day, our battle cry is, "I am created in God's spiritual image, born again through Christ's sacrifice, saved by God's grace, traveling with the Holy Spirit, one day to be arm in arm with Jesus. I am alive in Christ! Hallelujah!!"

You may say to yourself, "I'm happy with my life; why do I need Jesus?" Happiness is very fleeting—happy today, sad tomorrow; excited today, gloomy the next day. Happiness depends on events.

A man received a letter from the IRS which stated he had a refund coming of four thousand dollars (happiness). Two days later, another letter arrived telling him to disregard the first notice because he actually owed four thousand dollars (gloom).

You can decide to live in a state of peace because you have willed (given) your life to Jesus the Christ and your place in the heavenly realm has been bought and paid for! We don't live solely for the walk on this earth but are aware of the trip to come to our eternal home. Our earthly walk is not a destination but rather a part of our journey. Being born again allows us each day to ask, "Jesus, what are we going to do today?"

And when problems arise, to say, "Jesus, I can't wait to see how you, through the Holy Spirit are going to lead me through this!"

The joy of accepting Jesus will allow you to use gifts and talents you didn't even know you had! Pick a day; proclaim to the world, "This I claim as the day I fully accepted Jesus and was born again."

ILLUSTRATIONS

After years of wandering, Clint realized something important was missing from his life. He had an empty feeling and was drawn to visit a local church out of a sense of searching.

As he entered the church for the first time in his life, he was shocked—for people were dressing up in long robes with ropes around their waists and were putting on false beards and headdresses. One of the members who recognized a stranger said to Clint, "What better way to get to know us than to become a part of the mob."

No, it wasn't the choir, and no, they weren't going to lynch the preacher, but the church was reenacting the events leading up to the crucifixion of Jesus. Clint would be a part of the crowd that shouted, "Crucify Him, crucify Him!"

Hesitantly he agreed. Then the preacher rushed up to him and said, "The man who was supposed to be one of the thieves on the cross is sick. You aren't known here in the church, and it would be so effective. Will you play the part?"

Clint's brain was shouting no, but for some reason, his head was nodding yes. They showed him the cross where he would look on as Jesus died. As he stood there, a weak, empty feeling came over him. His first day in church ever, and he had gone from being drawn to see what Jesus could do for him, to a member of a mob scene, to thief on the cross.

But something was overwhelming him. He knew very well the feelings on the cross because, what the church didn't know, he had just been released from prison after serving ten years; he was in fact a real thief. Having been introduced to the Christian faith by the prison chaplain, could it be possible that in that church he could find a source of forgiveness that would release him from his sins? What could this Jesus have to do with him?

A question asked by many. This Jesus, who nearly two thousand years ago, made His way to the cross. As the play unfolded, Clint found himself being caught up in the event; this was all so very new. He almost felt like one of the people in the crowd—hopeful that Jesus could bring peace to their lives. He began to see in the story that Jesus was after the people's very soul. "Why, heck," he thought. "He's after mine too!"

All this time, Clint had done things his way. The thought of turning his life over to Christ never before entered his mind. Now, for the first time in his life, he began to sense emotions he didn't know he had. The fact that someone would willingly prepare to die so that those who called upon His name could have eternal life; it was overwhelming. Yet, Clint was feeling a little excited with these strangers who were quickly becoming friends.

The play was about to start, and then, as if fate hadn't done enough for one night, there was one more surprise. For someone called out, "Clint, bring the cross over here."

The cross, which he had not noticed, now loomed so large behind him. It was heavier than he thought, and he had to drape it over his back to carry it. It was a short distance to carry it. Only a few people were watching. Why did he feel so unworthy? Why did he feel that someone else should carry it? It wasn't a big cross. Why did it seem so large and heavy? Why did the walk seem so long?

Clint reflected, "A part of me wants to get it over with, to put it down. I feel very uncomfortable with it."

And now—to this man who had come for the first time to a church to see if he could find religion and release from his sins and peace in his spirit, who was part of a mob, selected to be a thief on the cross, and was now carrying the cross of Jesus—something else unexpected happened. Clint had taken the cross to the altar where it was needed at the same time a little child came into the sanctuary.

The child looked up, saw the cross, came over, and touched it. With penetrating, innocent eyes, the boy asked him, "Did Jesus really die on a cross like this?"

It was all he could do to fight back the tears. He said yes.

The little boy's face lit up as he began to comprehend, probably for the first time in his life, what Jesus has done for him.

Clint laid the cross down, fell on his knees, and sobbed.

It changes your life when you meet the Master, wouldn't you say?

* * * * *

We are never too old or too young to learn and to be used by God. A man was doing a story about an artist who had created a painting on an eighty-acre field. The best way to view this unusual artwork was from a plane.

The writer and his photographer spotted an old J-2 Piper Cub parked in the old man's backyard. They asked if he would fly them and the man agreed.

Flying at two thousand feet, the writer asked the pilot how long ago he got his pilot's license.

"I don't have any pilot's license," the old farmer told them. "I just found this thing wrecked out there, patched it up, and taught myself how to fly it."

It's never too late to grow, to learn, and to have new experiences. We don't know what tomorrow may bring, but we know God has a plan for each of us. If you are unhappy with a part of your life, maybe after a lot of prayer, God will show you that either He doesn't want you there or that you are there for the wrong reason. Maybe you are there not just to always receive but to give as well.

It's so sad to hear someone say, "I feel God is calling me to change, and I should, . . . but I can't."

And when asked why they can't, the answer is, "I don't know; I just can't."

What a pity that someone has that little trust in God. If He gives you the vision, He has already prepared the way, and Christ through the Holy Spirit will guide you. We walk in faith and belief in the stories of Scripture. We are disciples of Jesus because we have declared in our personal way that the story of who He is, is indeed true. It might not seem logical to the world and it might not always be popular, but our belief in Scripture shapes who we are, or at least it should.

A woman was driving down a busy street, and she was tailgating too closely the car in front of her. The car in front made an ordinary stop, but she couldn't and hit the bumper.

She immediately began to scream with unfriendly language, waving her hands and fists, giving all kinds of hand signals, and when the police who were just a few cars back saw this, they arrested her.

Later, they released her with an apology. They told her, "We saw your actions and heard your language, and then noticed the back of your car which had stickers saying, 'I love Jesus. What Would Jesus Do?' and 'I am a Christian.' We thought you stole the car!"

A true encounter with the Lord and Savior, Jesus the Christ, changes lives in such a way that, "What would Jesus do?" are not mere words but a standard for living. Do people know you are a Christian by the way you act or do you have to tell them?

* * * * *

I'm sure if we are honest, we have to admit we have all been tempted. I'm reminded of the story about a man who came forward at the close of every service during the rededication time and always prayed the same prayer. "Lord, take the spiderwebs of temptation out of my life."

The pastor, tired of hearing the same petition, knelt beside him at the altar one Sunday and prayed, "And, Lord, while you're at it, please kill that spider!"

Many times, we want a different result, but we keep doing the same thing. This week, identify one bad behavior you use and try to root it out of your system. I know you have at least one unless you want me to believe you're perfect.

You will find it goes much easier through prayer and a renewed commitment to Christ. I once had someone tell me, "Yes, that's what I do. My father was that way and his father also. That's just the way we are!"

But the person didn't say, "That's the way we have to be!"

It takes strength to change those negative things about us, but if you are willing, I believe the Holy Spirit of God can bring the force of Christ to bear and change will occur. Of course, the premise this is built upon is that you have to be willing.

Identify a negative behavior; are you willing?

* * * * *

Change is hard for some people. Often this is exacerbated by a lack of information.

A man arrived late for a board meeting at the church. Someone had brought up the need for a new chandelier in the sanctuary to add more light to the area. The latecomer caught the tail end of the discussion and rose to his feet to announce, "I am against it!"

He proceeded to give his reasons. "It costs too much, and besides, we don't have anyone who can play it. What we really need is more light in the sanctuary."

Sometimes people are quick to judge an idea before they have adequate information to make an informed decision. Change doesn't come easy for some people. Some church historians have said that when a church is standing still, it's dying and doesn't know it.

How about in your life? Are you open to the newness and freshness of ideas and thoughts that God can bring? Or is every idea or person who does not agree with your thinking just "stupid?" Sometimes, to do God's work, we have to get out of our comfort zone. We might even have to be with people we are not comfortable with. Gosh, could you handle that much religion?

PRAYER

Dear God, I come to You on this day with a grateful heart. Through Your grace, I have met the trials of the past week and celebrate that indeed nothing has been able to separate me from Your great love. It gives me comfort knowing that during my spiritual journey Your presence through the Holy Spirit is with me. Even when the world will try and deal me a blow, I will take comfort in my faith in You. For it is in the disappointments of life that the evil one will certainly try and make his presence known.

I pray that I will always receive the clearness of thought that will allow me to see his actions for what they are—an attempt to separate me from You. Help me to have the wisdom to know that things that come against me I can turn around and use to testify to my trust in you. For You are my deliverer from fear, worry, and confusion. You give me understanding that "This too shall pass."

If I am faithful, You will guide me through the trial and even use it to make me stronger. In this earthly journey, I may find peace with You in any storm. It is those times when I take my attention away from You that I begin to lose my way.

I ask for forgiveness for the times I have felt my joy and soul is safe only in my hands. For it is then that I am a target for pride, selfishness, fear, jealous behavior, as well as other destructive actions. Eternal God, guide me to seek the light of Jesus, the Risen Savior, so that others may see Christlike behavior in me.

Omnipotent God, I bring to You my sadness for the many in this world who suffer from health issues, effects of war, and being uprooted from their homes, those who are being cast into prison for their religious beliefs and who long to be free. Please strengthen the determination of freedom throughout the world and continue to look with favor upon our country that we may continue to be a beacon and example of freedom for the rest of the world.

May the conviction of Your Holy Spirit lead politicians to set aside political bickering and personal agendas to seek Your vision for this great nation. May I be called to look for and to find opportunities each day to show my love for You. These things I ask in the name of Jesus, the Risen Savior, who taught the prayer saying, "Our Father . . ."

What Would It Take for You to Do It Another Way?

SERMONETTE

Matthew 18:1-4

We now need to discuss a topic very upsetting to many people. This word makes preachers go weak in the knees and church members belligerent! That word is "change."

When a new idea is introduced in the church, responses sound like, "We don't do it that way here!" Or "If it isn't broke, don't fix it!"

Change is hard. Would you consider going to the hairdresser or barber and saying, "Give me a new style, a complete change. Be creative; make it different."

A new couple paid their first worship service visit to a church I served. I met them, gave them a tour of the church, told them I would check on them after the service, and I did. They told me they would never come back! I asked why. "Was it the sermon?"

They said no, they liked that. But they were seated, and a church member came up to them and said, "You are in my seat! I have sat in that seat for thirty years, so now move!"

Change has to do with your comfort zone; exchanging something familiar with something not so familiar is very difficult for some people. There is fear that change might turn out to be worse than the present circumstance (the devil we know instead of the angel we don't know).

Jesus talked about change but He called it repentance. Repent means to change direction and go 180 degrees from where you are now, not 360 degrees or you would make a circle and be back where you started.

To Him, repentance is more than a change of mind or feeling sorry over one's action; it's returning to God by deliberate action. This word often brings big sinful things to mind such as murder, arson, or robbery. Nowhere in the New Testament account of Jesus do we find Him rating sin. He never said, "Murder is a ten, gossip a five, lying a three." A sin is a sin!

And what is a sin? Anything we do which is not pleasing to God and separates us from God's care, and presence. Sin starts with an evil desire, then rationalization (without prayer), followed by action. I mean, what harm is a white lie going to do? Telling that dirty, racist joke—people laughed, didn't they? Instead of doing the devil's bidding and making fun of someone, seek to change and become uplifting instead.

A preacher was asked to do a funeral for the man the town referred to as no-good. Everyone talked about this, and the opinion was, "We have the preacher now; there is no way he can say something good!"

The day of the service arrived. The preacher stood up. All was quiet. He said, "You might not know this but Ned could play the best harmonica you ever heard!"

Maybe a change is necessary for you to find God's purpose, vision, and direction. Jesus said to repent (change). "I am the way" (John 14:6).

In repentance, we don't stay in "what was" but rather move to what "will be." It gives freedom to find peace, excitement, and blessings. Remember, Jesus came to comfort the afflicted and afflict the comfortable! Change is not easy. Talk to God and discern if some change is needed in your life's spiritual journey. Are you up for an exciting change?

ILLUSTRATIONS

A woman attended her son's track meet. On the fourth and final lap of the mile run, everyone was clumped together except for the two front-runners, who were leading the pack. As the runners came toward the finish line, the crowd began cheering wildly.

Just then, she happened to look back, and there, hopelessly last, was a short, portly, kid who never should have walked a mile, let alone run one. His entire body was wobbling toward the finish line, and his bright red face was twisted in a kind of pain that made her wonder if death was near!

Suddenly, a frantic parent leaped down the bleachers to the railing around the track. She was obviously the poor boy's mother. She yelled at the top of her lungs, "Johnny, run faster!"

A look of hopelessness registered on Johnny's face. He had to be thinking, "Run faster? RUN FASTER? What am I, an idiot? What do you think the problem is here? I just forgot to run faster? I am running as fast as I can!"

I submit to you that life is like that sometimes—we do our best. We try as hard as we can. We prepare, we plan, we study, we resource, and in spite of it all, our efforts don't seem to get it done. Our best-laid plans are not good enough. It could be we left something out. If you make bread and forget something, like the yeast, it isn't going to turn out right. Prayer and listening for God's guidance is the yeast of life. Instead of trying to make your plan work by just running a little faster, why not search for God's plan? Maybe you are trying to do too much now. Your life could be cluttered with things that don't matter.

If you are "sick and tired of being sick and tired," try another way. The peace for which you are searching can only be found in the way of Christ seeking God's way. Don't run faster—run differently!

* * * * *

I am reminded of the man who didn't know what to buy his wife for her birthday. Setting out to shop for something different, he found the solution to his problem in a pet show. Here was a very rare and expensive talking bird—the Mexican "Wordy Bird."

He ordered it crated up and sent to his home with a note which read, "Happy birthday, darling."

A few hours later he called his wife to find out whether his present had arrived and how she liked it. "Just fine," came the reply. "It's in the oven right now."

The husband was appalled and astonished. "But, that was a smart and very rare talking Wordy Bird," he pleaded.

"If it was such a smart bird," she said sweetly, "then why didn't it speak up and say something?"

* * * * *

A suitor wrote some seven hundred love letters proposing marriage over two years. His persistence finally paid off and brought results. The girl became engaged to the mailman who regularly delivered all those letters.

Things do not always turn out as we expect.

* * * * *

I read about a children's pageant where the innkeeper was played by a boy named Ralph who had very much wanted to play the role of Joseph. He didn't get the part and had refused to be part of the program, but, his mother and the director insisted that Ralph do his duty and be part of the pageant. So he was the innkeeper. But Ralph decided on revenge.

When that part of the pageant occurred in which Joseph inquired about a room, Ralph grinned and announced, "Come on in. We've got plenty of room."

The audience, especially Ralph's mother and the director gasped. Joseph and Mary were stunned. They expected to be turned away. Obediently they walked into the inn. But the young man playing Joseph was equal to the occasion.

He looked around, turned to the audience, and said, "Hey, this place is a dump. We'd rather stay in the stable."

What would life be without such surprises? We all have something in life that surprises us occasionally.

Adlai Stevenson, the much-respected politician, told this one on himself. He said that when he served in the Agricultural Adjustment Administration, he wrote a marketing agreement for the walnut industry. That Christmas, the industry thanked him by sending him an enormous gunnysack full of packages of walnuts. This generous gift came forth at a very fortuitous time because Stevenson had not done his Christmas shopping.

Happily, he took these packages of walnuts and sent them to all his Washington friends. Then he made the awful discovery. In each of the individual packages was a card saying, "Merry Christmas from the walnut industry to Adlai Stevenson."

There are some surprises we could do without. Christmas, however, is not one of them. God comes into the world in the person of a tiny baby. Angels sing, shepherds rejoice, and the world is forever changed. That's one surprise the world is still coming to grips with.

* * * * *

A very familiar maxim tells us you can't judge where a person will end up by looking where he or she began. We find this to be true in the story of Harry and Ada Mae whose first child, Sandra, was born in El Paso, Texas.

When they brought Sandra home, it was to their small adobe ranch which had no electricity or running water. With such limited resources, one would have thought that Sandra's future was not bright. But, most of us know her today as Sandra Day O'Connor, the first woman Supreme Court justice in the United States. You can't judge a person by their beginnings.

When Jesus was born in Bethlehem of Judea, it was not to affluent parents, and yet, He grew up to change the entire relationship between God and humanity. Are there any judgmental categories or prejudices which are affecting your walk as a true disciple of Jesus the Christ?

PRAYER

Almighty God, it is with great joy that I recognize Your presence and gracious manner in which You have provided for me. When so many of Your loved ones worldwide deal with health issues, face-to-face encounters with terrorists and different atrocities, living conditions below what I would call primitive, where many are displaced from their homes by war, seeking shelter in refugee camps, You have graced me with abundance.

May I see Your gifts not as an entitlement but an opportunity to reach out to those the world has made less fortunate. May I concentrate less on political correctness and more on generosity, unity, and sharing. Less on gender and skin color and more on being Christlike, loving, and forgiving. Sometimes when I'm made aware of conditions in the world, I wonder what I can do to bring about even a small change. Yet, change takes place when individuals, one by one, become more dedicated to the cause.

May I become more dedicated to the cause of Jesus the Christ. Give me the opportunity to spread the gospel good news story by my words, actions, and deeds. For You have told me in the words of Scripture, to whom much is given, much will be required. Take away from me excuses that draw me to activities and not worship; excuses which keep me from following Your will which I feel You placing on my heart; excuses which allow me to be self-centered and not Holy Spirit-centered. And may I continue my journey with enthusiasm and seek more vigorously Your vision.

Challenge me with new avenues of service to the lost, the least, and the lonely. I have so much to be thankful for—help me to show my love and appreciation through the time and effort I take, in various ways, to worship You. And when I or loved ones deal with difficulties, let Your Spirit of strength and peace be present. Strengthen our faith to always be able to pray, "Thy will be done."

I continue to lift up leaders worldwide and pray You will give them righteous hearts and behavior pleasing to You. These things I ask in the name of Jesus the Living Christ Who taught the prayer, "Our Father . . ."

Is Fear Robbing You?

SERMONETTE

Luke 12:4-12

There are some people old enough to remember the time of the hysteria in our country concerning the fluoridation of our water. People were reporting to the authorities how this new fluoride was staining their dentures. One person complained how it caused a two-week headache. The only problem was, the process had not started! These people, and many others, were reacting in fear.

I believe we can define fear as being afraid of losing something comfortable or precious to us. If someone gained by inheriting $300,000, it would be unusual for them to exclaim, "I'm scared to death!" Or, if they had just paid off their house mortgage to say, "Now, I'm really afraid."

We could be afraid of losing our health or even losing our life. Fear can be a good thing. If you come out of your house to see a tiger standing on your walkway, fear and the ability to move fast might save your life. This instinct helped our forefathers when the woolly mammoth came after them.

The vast majority of our fears today, however, are not over real things. They are what professional medical staff call "paper tigers." We also know that this type of fear can rob us of many blessings. You might know some people who might be receptive to an invitation to visit church, but fear sets in. What if they get upset? What if they ask me to name all the books of the Bible! What if they think I'm too religious and I am *one of those*? What if . . .

This leads to the fear of making a mistake. In your growing up years, did you have to pay a penalty for even honest mistakes? As you look back, can you identify someone who, in a disagreement, was always right and you were almost always wrong or stupid or misinformed? Can you identify constant putdowns by someone trying to control you? Does it still bother you so much that even now you are hesitant to enter discussions because you're afraid to confront such behavior for the past will tell you, you will pay a penalty?

Being afraid to stand up for yourself and face paper tigers is a learned behavior; who taught you? Considering fear in general, can you imagine all the many blessings satan has found ways to deprive you of through fear?

I had a friend who would not drive a car over a bridge. She would be a passenger because she could shut her eyes! This is ridiculous you say, but how about your fears? Fear of being wrong, fear of not knowing what to say, etc., etc. If fear means we're afraid of losing something, what would it take to make the big jump and lose the fear? The vast majority of our fears have never happened and never will. But, during that time, fear has robbed you of so many blessings. If you're going to be all you can be, you're going to have to break out of some emotional prison you and others have put you in. You're going to have to learn to discern real tigers from paper tigers.

If it's your desire to be set free from fear, turn it over to God in prayer—let go and let God. Ask the Holy Spirit to guide you, and be prepared to act boldly! Today is the first day of the rest of your life; why let satan and the voices of the past continue to make you afraid? Declare now that your life is no longer controlled by the will of others but instead by the Risen Lord and Savior, Jesus the Christ!

One of the things Christ through the Holy Spirit will help you understand is that making mistakes is the way God's children learn. Due to the pressure you faced, you might have tried to keep the peace by always being perfect. I will wager all I own it didn't work! Let go of those shadows from the past. Sweep out those compartments of your being and ask Jesus to come and live there. Go to God in prayer, seek direction through Jesus, and ask that the Holy Spirit bring wisdom and strength. With these three aspects of God fighting for you, you have already won! Now, be bold! Go For It!

ILLUSTRATIONS

From personal experience, do you know the meaning of fear and how it feels? Do you know the difference between real and irrational fear? A young man in high school wanted to ask a young lady to go to a movie with him. He didn't have a fear that she would harm him, but he had a real, irrational fear of asking her for there was a good possibility she might say no. Besides, what would be the perfect words to use? Suppose her father answered the phone?

Suppose that satan has many fears that can be used against you. How about fear of a close relationship; fear of failing (why take a chance?); fear of making a mistake (so I won't even try); and the big one—change (if it isn't broken, don't change it). The majority of times, we don't even know where these irrational fears come from.

As part of her job, my friend was required to travel to different regions in the state. Before her trips, she mapped out the route to be sure there were no bridges to cross. She was petrified of driving across a bridge. She could ride in a car as a passenger, but she would freeze if asked to drive across the bridge. She could give no reason for the fear. An irrational fear caused her to drive out of her way to avoid a bridge.

Why not look at the irrational fears which are hindering your growth? There isn't a single one you can't conquer with the help of Jesus the Christ. Don't let irrational fear keep you from becoming the person God wants you to become. Jesus can give you the strength to overcome adversity, but it requires trust. Do you have enough?

* * * * *

During one Mother's Day rally event in a particular church, a little girl was to recite the Scripture she had memorized for the occasion. When she got up in front of the crowd, the sight of hundreds of eyes peering at her caused her to forget her verse. Every line she had so carefully rehearsed faded from her mind and she stood there unable to utter a single word.

In the front row, her mother was almost as frantic as the little girl. The mother gestured, moved her lips, trying to form the words for the girl, but it did no good. Finally, the mother in desperation whispered the opening line of the memorized Scripture, "I am the Light of the world."

Immediately the child's face lit up and a smile appeared as she said in a loud voice, "My mother is the light of the world."

* * * * *

Fear is generally not planned and makes us act in some unplanned ways. I like the story of the mountaineer who had been gone from home for over a week. When he came back home, his clothes were worn thin, and it was obvious he was exhausted. His wife put her hands on her hips and asked with suspicion, "Where have you been?"

"I went out in the woods to check the still," he replied, "and a great bear stepped out in front of me. I took off running ahead of him and finally lost him. I never ran so fast in all my life."

"But, that was a week ago," said the wife. "Where have you been since?"

"I've been walking back," he said.

* * * * *

Fear clutches my heart, and the future looks bleak. But my faith must not falter, and never grow weak. For whenever I am troubled and things become grim, I turn to Jesus my Lord and ask help of Him. He wipes away the troubles and burdens I bear. His compassion and mercy keep me safe in His care. When my wellspring of faith remains steadfast and true, the Lord loves and protects me in all that I do.

* * * * *

Fear will determine how we deal with life. It's like the two men riding a tandem bike up a long, steep hill. When they finally got to the top, the front bicyclist, sweat dripping from him, turned to the other rider and said, "Man, what a hill."

"Yeah," said his companion, "and if I hadn't kept the brake on, we could have rolled backward which I was afraid we would do!"

Fear can influence the way we lead our life. I wonder what fears might be within each of us which are keeping us from the blessings God has planned.

PRAYER

Dear everlasting and patient God, I do understand the difference between living *in* the world rather than living *of* the world. When things come upon me, I try not to respond as the world standards would have me do, but rather I seek Your standards. It's at times difficult, and I find myself giving into the harmful ways of the world which seem pleasant and satisfying. I find myself elevating my wants over other's needs, passing judgment in place of compassion and understanding, allowing my words to hurt instead of uplift. In ways I have not pleased You, I ask for forgiveness, wisdom to see my errors, strength, and the light of Jesus the Risen Christ to guide my path.

For in my heart, I know that true joy, peace, and sense of fulfillment can only be mine when I fully worship You every day. Help me to be on guard against the evil one's use of fear in my life. Help me to never fear stepping out in faith for the calls to action You place upon me. Satan will try and distract me from the path which leads to You. His weapon of fear will have me question my gifts and talents, worry about failure, and even question the soundness of such a course. Why reach out to a neighbor (you might

82

make them uncomfortable)? Why tell my family I love them (they might suspect my motive)? Why testify to my faith when the occasion presents itself (might be seen as overly religious and offensive)?

Satan will always have fears to keep me from the path You have for me. Let me not, through satan's fears, forfeit my blessings You wish to give me for actions in faith and trust. When I feel my action is encouraged by You, drive me above fear and into the realm of confidence. For when I place my trust in You above fear, You will provide the way for me to meet challenges successfully.

Dear God, as I rely more on the gospel good news story and the understanding that this life is but a journey, not a destination, guide me to travel a little lighter in Your company without all the *should, oughts*, and *fears*. Let me not miss the gorgeous sunrise or sunset, the song of a bird, the beautiful petals of a flower, and acts of caring. Turn my attention always to the inner peace of being more Christlike, to the joy of service, to the contentment of living a life dedicated to You. When unrest and fear seem to surround me, make me more in concert with You.

Heavenly God, so many of Your children are affected by disasters, illness, oppression. Be with each; bring Your comforting presence and the path of hope. Lead world leaders to seek Your path. These things I ask in the name of Jesus who taught the prayer saying, "Our Father . . ."

Is This a Name You Can Live With?

SERMONETTE

Acts 26:1-32

The Native American Indians had a very interesting way to name their children. The new mother would close her eyes and be led outside. She would open her eyes and name the baby after the first thing she saw, i.e. "Running Deer" or "Falling Rock."

Each of us has a given name, and we weren't involved in choosing that name. There is also another name you have, but you had to be involved and then accept it. You didn't have to complete an application, fill out papers, or earn a degree, but it still wasn't easy to achieve this name.

This accepted name should cause altered lifestyle or behavior changes. It most likely could cause you to examine the things you selfishly hold dear as opposed to helping the person down the street who is in need. When you live by this name, statements such as, "I am so stressed I don't know what to do," become "but God does and will show me the way through the Holy Spirit."

This name will lead to prayer, Bible reading (start with the New Testament Book of John) for strength and wisdom, and a stronger relationship with Christ. As a side note, don't let anyone tell you that you don't take anything with you when you die; you definitely take your relationship with Jesus the Christ. When we die and stand in God's presence, we hope to hear our accepted name called with the words, "Welcome home, good and faithful servant" versus, "What was your given name, and who are you?"

The name we accept is "Christian." We get the name by pouring out such things as pride, prejudice, judgments (shoulds and oughts) and taking in their place the full acceptance of Jesus the Christ as Lord and Savior, Jesus the Living Water. But as a Christian, you will not always get your way! Sometimes we ask Jesus through the Holy Spirit to take away things that negatively affect us, and the answer might be, "No. But I will show you how to overcome them."

Just because you are a Christian doesn't mean you'll always get a yes. There can very well be no's to help you grow and be prepared for the yes that comes later. When you accept the name Christian, you agree to live as Christlike as possible and strive to (among other things) rise above pettiness and accept the Christian life as a standard. One day, your journey on the earth will be over. If you have tried to live your life with one foot in the worldly ways and the other in the ways of Jesus, the question becomes: what do you want Jesus to call you?

ILLUSTRATIONS

A young boy was born with Down Syndrome. At first, he seemed to be a happy child, but he soon began to realize he was different from other children. They were unkind in their comments and, in many cases, were unaccepting of his differences. His mother, hoping for a better result, took him to a Sunday school class with other boys and girls his age. Unfortunately, his ways and actions were not readily accepted by the class.

During the Easter season, the teacher came up with a bright idea. She brought enough pantyhose containers, which looked like big eggs, for each child in the class to have one. The children were asked to go outside to find a representation of new life and put it inside the pantyhose container, then return to the classroom.

The teacher then opened them one at a time. One had a four-leaf clover, one a flower, but the last one opened was empty. Many children cried out that it wasn't fair and somebody messed up. The young boy whispered to the teacher that it was his egg and it was supposed to be that way.

As the children chastised him, he blurted out that it was empty because the tomb was empty. There was a silence over the Sunday school class. From that time on, the boy enjoyed a different relationship with each classmate.

He died at the beginning of the summer and was buried at the church. On the day of his funeral, his former classmates, with their teacher, entered the church, bearing not flowers but empty, egg-shaped pantyhose holders. Each one took turns laying the holder on the altar, and each one knew that the tomb of Jesus the Christ was empty.

The next time the urge comes to run somebody down for their differences, remember, in God's love—the tomb is empty.

* * * * *

A man in a Boston church had for some reason inflamed the anger of a woman in the church. This woman wrote poison pen letters to the man, and she was tireless in her efforts to build dissension against him in the church. After the unpleasant relationship had gone on over many years, quite unexpectedly, the woman moved to Arizona.

Many months later, the man received a letter from her saying simply she had a change of heart and was enormously sorry for what she had done to him and for the problems she had caused in church. She begged the man's forgiveness.

The man telegraphed her this message from the heart of a strong man: "Forgiven, forgotten, forever."

But see where it starts—you can't just start with forgetting; first must come genuine forgiveness. And if you do remember it, remember it as a celebration of how you were set free to forgive. Don't keep reliving the pain, but give deep thanks for the strength you received to move on. When you do remember, make it a positive experience.

* * * * *

As John Wesley rode across Hounslow Heath late one night, singing a favorite hymn, he was startled by a fierce voice shouting halt, while a firm hand seized the horse's bridle. Then the man demanded, "Your money or your life."

Wesley obediently emptied his pockets of the few coins they contained and invited the robber to examine his saddlebags, which were filled with books. Disappointed at the result, the robber was turning away when the evangelist cried, "Stop. I have something more to give you."

The robber, wondering at this strange call, turned back. Then Wesley, bending down to him, said in a solemn tone, "My friend, you may live to regret the sort of life in which you are engaged. If you ever do, I beseech you to remember this, 'The blood of Jesus Christ, God's Son, cleanseth us from all sin.'"

The robber hurried silently away, and the man of God rode along praying in his heart that the words spoken might be fixed in the robber's conscience.

Years later, at the close of a Sunday evening service with the people streaming from the large building, many lingered around the doors to see the aged preacher, John Wesley. A stranger stepped forward and earnestly begged to speak with Mr. Wesley. What a surprise to find that this man was the robber of Hounslow Heath, now a well-to-do tradesman in the city and, even better, a child of God and follower of Christ. The words spoken that night long ago had been used by God in that man's conversion.

Raising the hand of John Wesley to his lips, he affectionately kissed it and said in tones of deep emotion, "To you, dear sir, I owe it all."

Wesley replied softly, "Nay, nay, my friend, not to me, but to the precious blood of Christ, which cleanseth us from all sin."

The man had felt the touch of the Master. The question for us is do we know *about* Jesus or do we *know* Jesus? When can you say you met the Master?

* * * * *

Oscar Wilde, the Irish wit of the past century, author, and playwright, was not only a good writer but also a student of human nature. He loved stories. He liked to tell the story about the day the devil was traveling across the desert and happened upon a pack of imps, his followers, who were giving fits to a rather holy hermit but without success.

The sainted man shook off all their temptations and suggestions. Lucifer stood back only so long. Finally, after rubbing his chin and coming to certain conclusions about their approach, he said, "What you do is too crude and obvious. Step back." Then he whispered in the man of God's ear. "Your brother, less educated than you, has just been made bishop."

All of a sudden, the countenance of the hermit changed, and a malignant presence of jealousy clouded the once serene face of the saint. "Why, the very idea that my brother would be chosen over me!"

The devil looked at his demons and said, "Now that's the way I recommend you do it because it's all in the approach."

This is why the Christian relies on Jesus the Christ. The devil has many sly ways, and we aren't able to see him coming. But even at his best, he's no match for Jesus. We will always be safe if, when we hear any knock on the door of our heart, we let Jesus answer the door.

* * * * *

In the spring of 1959, an Air Force major entered a Texas mental institution for the second time. He had tried to commit suicide twice and had been arrested for forgery and robbery. For years, he had been drinking heavily, and his marriage had disintegrated. Yet only fifteen years before, he had been a model officer headed for a promising career. One momentous event precipitated the major's plunge.

He flew the lead plane over Hiroshima when the first atom bomb was dropped. Shortly after that, he began seeing throngs of Japanese men, women, and children chasing him in his dreams, and his own life began to collapse. The psychiatrist who treated him said the major was subconsciously trying to provoke punishment from society to atone for the guilt he felt over Hiroshima and other acts.

My friends, guilt, fear, and regret are sometimes greater problems than we are prepared to recognize. There's only one place these negative forces can be permanently unloaded—at the foot of the cross. This is where meaningful forgiveness takes place and the strength to overcome is received. Is there some event you continue to live with that is holding you back from becoming the whole person Christ would have you to be? He has the power you need; why not free yourself from these chains?

PRAYER

Dear Benevolent God, I come in prayer recognizing Your presence is always available to me. Through the ages from the beginning of time, Your Spirit has existed to guide, support, and counsel and is a mighty bulwark against the darkness and sinister ways of satan who travels to and fro across the land. His diabolical plan to separate me from You would have me walk my earthly journey relying only on my skills. The cunning ways of this fallen angel would have me believe that I am capable, on my own, of deciding between him and You as I deal with my life's complexities, temptations, or trials. His argument for why I should follow him sounds so soothing and promises to bring rewards as I put myself first in all matters.

But dear heavenly God, I know deep within my spiritual heart that his way leads to chaos, broken promises, and the anxieties and frustration of feeling alone and overwhelmed—all designed to lead me to despair. And yet knowing this, I still find myself trying to rationalize why I should engage in the behavior I feel he is behind.

I say things like, "Falling from God's grace this one time won't hurt!" Then it becomes easier to fall on the slippery slope of satan's lies. In these moments, embrace me with Your love that never fails. Call to me anew; prick my conscience reminding me of Your steadfast will to share all aspects of my life in an uplifting manner.

Scripture tells me that I cannot serve two masters, and I can't jump back and forth between You and bad behavior. In my decisions, give me the strength to choose You as my partner in life for You provide the needed wisdom, the right sense of direction, and the soothing but challenging presence of Your Spirit—turning the fear of newness and freshness into exciting avenues of growth. And when trials descend upon me, I know that trust in You will make me stronger, and faith will lead to victory in Your name.

In Your name, as I go through changes, enliven my heart ever more knowing that You are the rock upon which I stand. Let me stand against satan's negativity of why I can't, but celebrate with You by saying, "Yes, I can."

I will celebrate with You in the present but pray that You will excite me with the hope and joy of things to come if I am only faithful to You. For those I name to You in my heart, grant them measures of peace, healing, and trust. Increase their faith, as well as mine, to always pray, "Thy will be done."

All across the world, dear Lord, peace is an elusive factor, so many sinful desires of ideology, power, and corruption. I continue to pray for the softening of hearts and repentance of world leaders presently not seeking Your will. These things I ask in the name of the Risen Lord, my Savior Jesus the Christ who taught the prayer saying, "Our Father . . ."

Why Wait for the Storm?

SERMONETTE

Mark 11:22-25

Prayer has proven to be very effective in healing and general peace of mind. Jesus gave us the example of prayer. As things good and not so good come into our life, many times we decide to only use it in extreme circumstances. One is certainly encouraged to pray over problems, disappointments, setbacks in life, etc., but why wait until the troubles hit before praying?

Prayer can be offered up at any time for such things such as (1) Wisdom to stay the Christian course, (2) Strength to resist temptation, (3) Ways to be of service, not selfish ways, (4) Love, not hate, (5) Direction, not confusion, and (6) To thank God for the many blessings bestowed on you. Prayer should include not only problem solving but praise giving as well. There are many times when you shouldn't rely just on people for your sense of direction.

A woman went into the drugstore and told the druggist, "I want some Castor Oil and please disguise the taste."

He said, "I'll be glad to. Please be seated at the counter, and I'll bring you a soft drink while you wait."

He came back later and asked, "How was it?" Seeing her surprise, he said, "I disguised the double amount of Castor Oil in the drink!"

"You idiot," she screamed. "It was for my husband out in the car!"

We will not only have good times but there will be literal and figurative storms in our life. Some will be of our own making, some will not. Pogo, in the comic strips, says, "We have met the enemy, and it is us!"

When the disciples were with Jesus in a boat on the Sea of Galilee, a literal storm came up, and they were afraid. Jesus wasn't, and He calmed the waves. Storms that come into our life allow us to demonstrate faith and understanding that the Risen Lord, through the Holy Spirit, is going to get you through it and make something good out of it. But you should feel this assurance through the practice and foundation of prayer in your life. Storms and disappointments will come. Will the next one find you prayerfully prepared? And when it comes (not if), where will your focus be? Will it be, "This is so unfair. Why me?" or will it be, "Let's turn it over to Jesus so He can make something better out of it."

The storm is coming; why not get into the boat with Jesus and be prepared when it comes? It's good to pray in the storm, but why wait? Why not now?

ILLUSTRATIONS

Oh, it was a horrible feeling. The storm was approaching with thunder and lightning, and I was far from home. In fact, I was in a huge field with a large tree in the middle, and I decided to hide beside the tree. There was a clap of thunder, and the tree burst into flames. Then I woke up. What a dream! What a storm! My heart felt as if it would bounce right out of my chest.

I had read just that day about the disciples and storms on the Sea of Galilee. Not only did they know about storms of nature, but they also were aware of storms of life. They were aware that, no matter how scary the storms of life can be, Jesus is able to get us through them.

At no time did Christ tell us that believing in Him would keep us from ever having storms in our lives. In fact, the opposite is true. Jesus told us we would experience disappointment, hurt, pain, and stress. Many people learn this sad news and become despondent. They fail to concentrate on the bright side, knowing that no matter how awful things get, Jesus, The Holy Spirit, and God are available

92

to get us through. By relying on this team, we come out on the other side much stronger. The plan as outlined in Scripture is not to shield us but to use adversity to strengthen us. The next time a storm of life hits, where are you going to find your peace and security? I hope it's not under a tree in the middle of a field.

* * * * *

What do you do when you have "giants" to face? It's like a certain father who listened as his son told him about his first serious conflict at school.

He had been picked on by three bullies who punched him and knocked him off his bike as he was riding home. The bullies had made life difficult for the boy, and he told his father that they threatened to do more harm the next day. The boy was greatly disturbed; he didn't know what to do.

That evening, the father taught his son some basic techniques on how to defend himself. Together they explored all the possibilities. The father worked hard to build up his son's self-confidence. The next morning, the father and son prayed together. And with a reassuring embrace and a handshake, the father smiled confidently and said, "You will make it alright."

With that assurance, the boy got on his bike and rode off to school. What the son didn't know was that the father followed him in the car that day. He stayed just far enough behind to remain out of sight but close enough to come to his son's assistance if needed. If there was trouble, the father would be there.

The son might have thought he was all alone, but his father was behind him. When we face our giants, just knowing that God is with us, like that father was with the boy, is a great comfort. We can face all sorts of giants when we know that God is with us.

* * * * *

When you consider walking hand-in-hand with God, what does that really mean? God doesn't literally offer His physical hand, but

He does offer, through the real and present Holy Spirit, a constant presence. When the storms of life come and we stumble, God is there.

When you walk with a young child and they hold your hand, if they trip, they may not be strong enough to keep a grip on your hand, and they might fall.

If you hold their hand, they might trip, but your grip will be strong enough to keep them from hitting the ground.

When we allow God to hold our hand, our spirit, our trust, we may still stumble, but with God on our side, we will never fall into the clutches of the evil one.

Through temptation, you might stumble, but through faith in God, by the Holy Spirit in the name of Jesus the Christ, you will be lifted up when storms of life come your way. What presence is holding your spiritual hand?

PRAYER

Dear heavenly God, as the seasons of weather change from winter to spring, I am joyful over the nature of Your creation. I am also mindful that as changes occur, Your love for Your children never changes. Whether I'm experiencing rain, snow, or sun, to experience the warmth of Your presence is a vital part of my being.

I am also aware that in the seasons of my life there are joyous times, times of fellowship, success, and well-being. Help me to see You through the Risen Christ in times of celebration. For as Jesus graced a wedding at Cana, so too can His presence be found on days when I feel uplifted and satisfied. And when I concentrate more fully on making His ways my ways, I know I will find gentleness and humbleness in a season of contentment found only through Him.

But dear omnipotent God, as I make my journey through my years of life, I am aware that the season of dark clouds, unsettling events, health issues, loss of loved ones, and other trials of life may well come my way. Let it be on my heart that You are a God for these events as well. May I feel the warmth of Your love that lets me know that by being faithful to You, even these trials will be used to strengthen and prepare me for a better day.

For Loving God, I desire a closer relationship with You in the name of Jesus the Risen Christ through the presence of the Holy Spirit. I ask for forgiveness in those times I did not follow Your will. When the dark side tries to lead me toward selfish, hurtful ways, direct me to the path of service and love. Even when things I can't change come upon me that I feel are so unfair, impart to me the ability through Christ to, "Let go and let God." And then help me to be vigilant for the ways each aspect of Your love will appear.

For those I lift up to You in my heart, You know the season of their life. Grant measures of peace, healing, and trust, and increase their faith, as well as mine, to always pray, "Thy will be done."

All across this world, dear God, peace is an elusive desire. So many desires of ideology, power, and corruption get in the way. I continue to pray for a softening of hearts, no matter how hard, and repentance on the part of world leaders not presently seeking Your will. These things I ask in the name of Jesus, who will one day return and judge all behavior and who taught the prayer, saying "Our Father . . ."

Why Are You Blaming Me?

SERMONETTE

Philippians 2:12-18

The presence of evil in our world is a real thing, and for those who follow this path, the story does not turn out well, especially in the long run. Jesus took on satan in the story of His temptation. This story in Scripture is important to us as it shows what kind of Messiah we follow. It also points out the main objective of evilness—to separate us from following the love of God, the teachings of Jesus, and the presence of the Holy Spirit.

Jesus showed in the way He handled these temptations that He would not: (1) Use His power for His own needs (turns stones to bread), (2) Do extraordinary things to get attention (throw Himself off the high point of the Temple so angels could catch Him), and (3) He would not compromise with the devil (worship me and I will give you everything). This last point is where many Christians start down the wrong path.

The devil doesn't have to trick you. He just presents you with an alternative set of actions tailored to help you draw away from the "narrow path" and enhance your pleasure. Then we rationalize it. "I'll laugh at this dirty or racial joke this time. Besides, I want to be popular with this group. God will understand."

That's true; God does understand! And as a part of our rationalization, we begin to look for someone or something to blame when things don't go well. Adam ate the forbidden fruit; he could have said no. He blamed Eve; she blamed the snake. They lost their point of reference, similar to the New Testament story of

Peter walking on the water (Matthew 14:22-31). As long as Peter kept his attention on Jesus, he was successful but when he looked down and concentrated on the rough water, he started to sink.

When you lose your point of reference and follow non-Christian behavior, things around you will begin to sink. You then will be given the greatest lie: "It's not your fault!"

The cunning one is very wily in that he picks his opportunity, and if he was willing to take on Jesus, be assured he will take you on and test you. Evil is real and not an illusion.

What is our defense? We can follow the lead of Christ and (1) Live on the word of God (the parts you haven't read won't help you), (2) Believe and have faith in the existence of God, Jesus the Christ, and the Holy Spirit. They are equally available to you and have a proven track record of being able to beat evil, and (3) Worship and serve God only. In other words, seek God through the path of Jesus in all you do. Let the spiritual uplifting presence of Jesus be your reference point. It's still a good thing to ask yourself, "What would Jesus do?"

When you leave Jesus out and bring other solutions in and things go wrong, are you comfortable with, "Hey, it's not my fault"?

ILLUSTRATIONS

I'm reminded of the farmer's son who decided to get married. His father said to him, "John, when you get married, your liberty is gone."

The boy replied that he did not believe this. The father said, "I'll prove it to you. Catch a dozen chickens, tie their legs together, and put them in the wagon. Hitch up the two horses to the wagon and drive them to town. Stop at every house you come to and, wherever you find the woman is boss, give her a chicken. You'll give away all your chickens. However, if you come to a house, and the man is the boss, give him a horse."

The boy accepted the proposition and drove to town. He had stopped at every house and had given away ten chickens when he came upon a house and saw an old man and his wife standing out on the front lawn. He called to them and asked, "Who is the boss here?"

The man said, "I am."

Turning to the wife, the boy said, "Is he the boss?"

The woman replied, "Yes, he's the boss."

The boy asked them to come down to the street. He then explained his reason for asking and told the man to pick out one of the horses.

The old man and the old lady looked over the horses carefully, and the husband said, "I think the black horse is the better of the two."

The wife then said, "I think that bay horse is in every way better. I would have chosen him."

The old man took another careful look at the bay horse and said, "I guess I'll take the bay horse."

The boy smiled and said, "No, you won't. You'll take a chicken."

There are times in our life when we want that black horse or something else really bad, and God says no and sends a chicken. Isn't it interesting how sometime later we see we really did need the chicken?

* * * * *

An elderly gentleman was out walking with his young grandson. "How far are we from home?" he asked the young boy.

The boy answered, "Grandpa, I don't know."

The grandfather asked, "Well, where are we?"

Again, the boy answered, "I don't know."

Then the grandfather said good-naturedly, "Sounds to me as if you're lost."

The young boy looked up at his grandfather and said, "Nope, I can't be lost. I'm with you."

Ultimately that is the answer to our lostness also. We can't be lost if God is with us.

* * * * *

I heard recently about an elderly man whose father was a Baptist preacher, and when he was young, they struggled with a very meager income to make ends meet. But no matter how small the amount, his father always gave 10% tithe. He said the children fussed because there were only beans on the table, and his father was sending 10% to the home office.

The beauty of it, as he remembers, is that they never missed a meal, always had a roof over them, and money seemed to come at just the right time from the strangest places.

Could you say today, "Even if I lost all that I own and have, God will provide"? That's God's promise—do you believe it?

* * * * *

Let me tell you the story about a man named Willis Moore. Willis recalls that his grandmother always ate cold grits. Now she preferred them hot but it was her priorities that caused her to eat them cold. Willis fondly remembers how his grandmother cooked a hot breakfast—fresh farm eggs, crisp bacon, homemade jelly, biscuits, and bowls of hot grits.

While the family was eating breakfast, Grandmother led devotions to the family. When she prayed, everyone stopped eating and bowed their heads. Afterward, everybody cheerfully joined in the table conversation while finishing the breakfast meal.

"Only then," Willis remembers, "did Grandmother start to eat cold grits." Willis remembers those special mornings and the example of his grandmother. At that time, it didn't seem all that important, but as years rolled on, he came to recognize the significance of those cold grits.

"Spiritual formulation," he writes, "is the memory of Grandmother putting God first at breakfast." Who would you say was instrumental in making God real to you?

But we must remember we don't get to heaven on Grandmother's coattails. Accepting Christ is a decision each person must make. We can't say, "Mom and Dad, who are Christians, took me to church. Therefore, I am saved."

Our spiritual salvation is something we have to do for ourselves. And it really is all or nothing. Are you still trying to play in the middle?

* * * * *

When you honestly seek the will of God, God will empower you and lead you to peace. Dwight L. Moody, the famous evangelist, once demonstrated this empowerment.

"Tell me," he said to the audience, "how can I get the air out of this fragile glass I have in my hand?"

One man said, "Suck it out with a pump."

The evangelist replied, "That would create a vacuum and shatter it."

Finally, after many futile suggestions, Moody picked up a pitcher of juice and filled the glass. "There," he said. "All the air is now removed."

He then explained that victory for the child of God doesn't come by working hard to eliminate destructive thoughts and worries but rather by allowing the Holy Spirit to take control with full possession.

PRAYER

Dear God, as I consider the awesomeness of who You are, the magnitude of creation, the sustaining power of Your love, the Keeper of my heavenly home, Your greatness and power can seem to be far distant from me. And then I'm caught up in the message of the world that if I want anything done right, I have to do it myself, as there is no one to help who can be trusted.

The sinister nature of this world would have me travel alone, unprotected, and fearful. As I journey here on my earthly home, the main purpose of the evil one is to separate Your children from You and Your great love. Your word in Scripture tells me of the great love You have for Your creation, even to the point of Jesus suffering and dying on the cross to provide a means of salvation. How You sent the Holy Spirit and have shown in the biblical stories how You seek a close relationship with believers and continue to seek the lost lamb.

I pray that Your presence will be more pronounced in my life so that I can consider You a partner in my life's decisions and not face the world alone. The further I pull from You, I experience a feeling of not being completely at peace, of fleeting happiness, not real, lasting joy, a feeling that—in all I have—something, a noticeable part, is missing—contentment.

Dear Caring God, You have created me in Your spiritual image and given me the path to Your love. May I spiritually understand that any distance between You and me is my doing. Forgive me when I fail to make the enrichment of our relationship my top priority. Give me spiritual ears to hear You calling and not be caught up in the tempter's snare. Open my eyes to wisdom and insight that I may understand what I am missing and how my life can be enhanced even more with a commitment of full trust and faith in You. How the peace that passes all human understanding may be mine when You are the center of my thoughts and actions.

Thank You for loving me so that I may experience, to a degree, the tranquility of what heaven is like during my earthly journey. I have loved ones and friends on my heart because of their struggles. Bring peace and, in Your will, healing. May each person draw closer to You in faith and trust. Give me what I need to take to them a message of hope. Guide men and women of righteous faith to withstand and defeat the forces of evil. May the Holy Spirit lead world leaders to follow Your path. These things I ask in the name of Jesus the Christ who taught the prayer saying, "Our Father . . ."

Is It Best Not to Know?

SERMONETTE

2 Thessalonians 2:5-12

Jesus said, "I tell you the truth . . ." and we are faced with one of two decisions: (1) Jesus was truthful and always told the truth, or (2) He was a liar. We can't pick and choose. Either they are true or they are not. We can't say, "These words of Jesus I believe, and I will make my lifestyle fit them. However, these other words of Jesus feel very uncomfortable, so I will overlook them."

Either you can count on all of Jesus's words, or you can't count on any of them! Jesus was very clear when He said, "I am the Light of the World" (John 8:12). We try and make religion complicated but it's quite simple: (1) Believe the words of Christ, or (2) listen to and follow the voices of the world.

Jesus, just like a present-day human shepherd, leads the sheep but does not drive them. The sheep know the shepherd's voice. But unfortunately, many people hear another voice from the world which leads to (1) pride, (2) haughtiness, (3) hate, (4) selfishness, (5) prejudice, and (6) fear. Then the decision is made not to read the Bible, especially the New Testament, because we would no longer have the excuse, "I didn't know." Next time you get caught speeding, try and tell the judge, "I didn't know I shouldn't speed!"

Besides, if I read the Scripture, it might come into conflict with what I want to do. However, how do I know if my action is pleasing to Christ or to the world? One of the best tests I've come across is to ask yourself, "How would I act if Jesus was standing beside me?"

In the Book of John, Jesus said, "I love my sheep so much I will lay down my life in order that those who believe in me shall have life everlasting." Do you accept that as truth? Is this belief shown in your actions, words, deeds, and testimony to others? The path to your heavenly home is not lined with excuses or half-hearted beliefs based on convenience. Is it time to free yourself from the voices of the world?

And as an afterthought, the only part of the Bible that will help you is the part you know about from your readings (For insight, read your Bible, beginning with the New Testament Book of John).

Now for the question—if you believe that Jesus always told the truth, are you going to live by those words, or are you going to spend time looking for ways around them?

ILLUSTRATIONS

There's a famous painting which shows the devil and a man in a chess match. All of the pieces for the man are gone except for the king, queen, and one little rook. The devil has him cornered, and he has a smirk on his face to symbolize what has happened. There are no more moves available to the man—the king has nowhere to go.

As part of the bargain, the devil gets the man's soul if the man loses. The devil is just waiting for the man to acknowledge the checkmate.

In an actual situation, a tour group went through the art gallery some years ago and, after the guide told the group how much this picture cost, who painted it, etc., they moved on. But nobody noticed that when the group moved on, one person stayed right there in front of that painting and kept staring and pacing back and forth. The man kept looking at the painting, and he kept looking at the painting. The group had moved and was two corridors away when all of a sudden, coming through those marble halls, they heard this man hollering at the top of his lungs, "It's a lie! It's a lie! The king has another move!"

Nobody knew that the man was the reigning international chess champion from Russia. As a Master, he could see that there was another move for the king. And the same thing is true when it comes to the King of kings, Jesus the Christ. For when it seems hopeless and that the devil has us with nowhere to turn, Jesus always has another move. For when we are open and silent and look with anticipation, then across our hearts will break the wonderment of it all—the joy of feeling and knowing that we are saved and no matter what, on behalf of God's children, the King always has another move!

* * * * *

Billy Graham was speaking in the San Jose area and on the closing day told this story. It seems there was a strong man who traveled with the circus. One of his most impressive stunts was to take an orange and squeeze every last drop of juice out of it. Then he offered $1,000 to anyone who could manage to squeeze as much as one additional drop from it. He went from town to town making the offer, but no one was able to win the $1,000 from him.

Then one day he came to a small town in California and made his demonstration of juice-squeezing ability and offered the challenge. A small, thin man came forward and said he's like to take a try at the challenge. He took the crushed orange and proceeded to squeeze six more drops of juice from it. The strong man was amazed. He could hardly believe his eyes. He asked the man how he was able to do this.

The man shrugged and said, "Oh, I'm the treasurer of the Methodist church and we do this all the time!"

* * * * *

Emotions, feelings—up and down, down then up. In a book of fiction, an author once tried to describe how the angels looked down and watched God's early creation of man and woman as they lived their lives methodically on earth, and the angels weren't having any fun. So they went to God and requested that God give humans emotions.

God did, and the angels haven't stopped laughing since.

A humorous story about a man who was drafted into the army. He became unhappy and dissatisfied and developed a quite disconcerting habit. As he walked along each day, he kept picking up pieces of paper, saying aloud, "That's not it."

This went on for about six months. Such bizarre behavior was finally brought to his superiors. They ordered him to report to the company psychiatrist. The psychiatrist asked, "What's wrong with you? What's your problem?"

The man had a baffled expression on his face as he asked, "What problem? I don't have a problem."

The psychiatrist said, "Well, there has to be something wrong with you. It's been reported to me that you keep going around all over the base picking up pieces of paper and you keep saying, 'that's not it, that's not it.' Now tell me just what is it you're looking for?"

The man said, "I don't know. I just don't know. I just don't seem to be able to find it."

The psychiatrist consulted with colleagues and told the man, "I think your problem is serious, and I'm going to give you a medical discharge."

When the psychiatrist handed the discharge papers to him, the man shouted, "This is it. This is it. This is the paper I was looking for."

You're up; you're down. Happiness is fleeting and depends on circumstances. However, no matter the circumstances, joy is everlasting. For joy tells us we are God's children created in the spiritual image of God, saved by Christ's gift and our acceptance of Him as Lord and Savior, protected by the ever-present Holy Spirit. Are you willing to settle for fleeting happiness or do you walk in the peace of pure joy?

* * * * *

Have you ever met someone who is a real worrier? I mean someone who has taken this art to the highest pinnacle, where it occupies most of their time. They have so many worries that they have to categorize them to make sure they all get "worried over." If one gets settled, there is a scramble to replace it with at least one more.

Now, here is the strange part—from the long list, only a few of the worries materialize. And most of these few appear without the intensity expected. Also, try as they might, the worrier is unable to think of all the things which do actually happen to them. Therefore, they worry over things that don't happen and don't worry over things that catch us off guard and do happen. The question arises—how accurate are our worries and are they worth the effort?

It's said that worry is similar to an old man with a bent head carrying a load of feathers which he thinks are bars of lead. Or it's like a rocking chair that takes a lot of effort but goes nowhere. Someone else quipped, "We used to take life with a grain of salt. Now we take it with five milligrams of Valium."

How many people have you ever heard say, "I cured my problem by worrying over it"? How about in your life? Can you name a time when worry solved a problem for you? I've met people who worry if they don't have anything to worry about. And they are most often very unhappy people. Always seeing the glass half empty will only cause a person to feel worse. Why not turn it over to God in constant prayer and joy in watching how God turns it around for a blessing? Next time you sense yourself worrying over something, pause, pray, and ask yourself—WHY?

PRAYER

All-loving and ever-present God, I talk with You today recognizing my need to be spiritually connected to Your grace and love. I open my spiritual heart to Your very presence. In the last days, my busyness may have kept me from honoring You by my words, actions, and thoughts. Please forgive my inattentiveness to You. Strengthen my desire to draw closer to You as I strive to be more Christlike.

In Jesus the Christ, You allow us, through the written Word, to see one who lived His life seeking Your will in all things. Guide me to be so inclined to pattern my way of life on His example as I interact with family, friends, and even the stranger. Most Caring God, I am reminded of the humiliation, suffering, and death of Jesus as He took upon Himself the sins of the world so that I can call Him Lord and Savior and take my place one day in Your heavenly home. For although not perfect, I am uplifted by Jesus's words, "I go to prepare a place for you."

Faith was made perfect when the tomb was found to be empty. Death could not hold Him in the grave, and my hope is alive for death will not be able to hold my spirit captive. Even as I continue on my life's journey, for whatever time is allowed, I take comfort in the understanding that the Spirit is available to always lead me along the path of peace and fulfillment. Christ's words and actions give me strength, and Your inspired Word in Scripture gives me wisdom and direction.

May the gospel good news story so overwhelm me that I will experience a repentant heart. May the way to salvation bring tears as I revel in Christ's gift to me. In the love of Christ, guide me to a closer walk with You and give me courage through the Holy Spirit to take that path. Suit a blessing to those I name in my heart. Guide world leaders to strive for peace. These things I ask in the name of Jesus who taught the prayer saying, "Our Father . . ."

It Is Such a Fleeting Thing

SERMONETTE

Romans 13:8-14

A patient was called to see the doctor about test results. When the patient arrived, the doctor told him, "I have good news and bad news."

The patient said, "Give me the good news first."

"You only have one day to live," said the doctor.

"Good Lord!" exclaimed the patient. "What could be worse than that?"

"Well," said the doctor, "I was supposed to tell you that yesterday!"

Time is a treasure. If you run out of money, you might change that. But if you run out of time, game over! And whether you are good or evil, rich or poor, man or woman, you only get twenty-four hours in each day. During that day, you have a lot of discretionary time. You make a lot of decisions on how to use that time. We say too many times, "I have to," when we should say, "I choose to."

When we say, "I choose to," we have to take responsibility. But to say, "I have to, don't blame me, I wasn't in control. They made me do it," is transferring responsibility.

"I had to take Aunt Mae to the doctor." No, you didn't! I don't care what your motivation was, you didn't have to take her; you choose to take her. There is only one thing you have to do—die! You don't have to pay taxes; you can refuse to pay and go to jail. Most of the things we do each day we decide to do; no one forced us to act that way.

And the things we didn't do were also our decisions. No one made you not pray or read Scripture; you decided against this. "But I had to watch that program on the History Channel." No. You choose between the two. And what did you have to do after that so you couldn't pray?

Many times we find competing interests for our time, especially in events such as Christmas. At this time, there are two celebrations: the Christmas of Santa Claus and the Christmas of the birth of Jesus the Christ. During this and other Christian events, if you start to say, "I have to do . . . ," pause and say, "I choose to do . . ."

Then ask yourself, "What did I decide to do today that will reflect Christlike behavior?" Deciding to use your treasure of time to follow the world might make you happy for a while. But deciding to use that treasure in Jesus's name to do it God's way will give you everlasting peace and the salvation of your soul. As you use your precious time, be aware of how you are choosing to use it. Tomorrow, if you are given twenty-four hours, how will you choose to use them?

ILLUSTRATIONS

A little boy was told by his doctor that he could save his friend's life by giving blood. The six-year-old child was near death, a victim of a disease from which the boy had made a marvelous recovery two years earlier. Her only chance for recovery was a blood transfusion from someone who had previously conquered the illness.

"Steven, would you like to give your blood for Mary?" asked the doctor.

The boy hesitated. His lower lip started to tremble. Then he smiled and said, "Sure, Doc. I'll give my blood for my friend."

As his blood siphoned into Mary's veins, one could almost see new life come into her tired body. The ordeal was almost over when Steven's brave little voice broke the silence, "Say, Doc, is it about time for me to die?"

It was only then that the doctor realized what the moment of hesitation, the trembling lip had meant earlier. Little Steven thought he was giving all his blood to his friend and was giving his life. And at that moment, he had made his great genuine decision of love.

We are reminded in Scripture that Jesus did give it all up for us. Jesus loves to be the Lord of our lives. Can we give up the self-centered ways of the world to allow this to happen?

* * * * *

Isn't it interesting how things can go wrong sometimes and end up not as we planned?

In a small Midwestern town one Christmas, a pageant was being given in the local church. The name of the pageant was The Bethlehem Star. At each of the practices, thirteen children walked across the stage, each one carrying a letter of the alphabet to spell out Bethlehem Star. But on the night of the production, the Star bearers got turned around and went in backward, so the church put on a production titled Bethlehem Rats. Everyone took it in stride and good jest. Even the pastor commented, "At least the bishop wasn't here."

As another example, after a man had his car radio stolen twice, he decided to invest in a removable radio. When he entered a shopping mall while doing his Christmas shopping, he felt secure at last because he had taken his radio with him. When he came out of the last store, he felt good. He knew this time no one could have stolen the radio. Imagine how he felt when he discovered his car radio wasn't stolen, but his car was!

Is there anything in this world we can count on? Yes, there is God's love and the ever-presence of the Holy Spirit. But you already knew that, didn't you?

* * * * *

A few years ago at the Seattle Special Olympics, nine contestants, all physically or mentally disabled, assembled at the starting line for the 100-yard dash. At the gun, they all started, not exactly in a dash, but with a relish to run the race to the finish and win; all that is except one boy who stumbled on the asphalt, tumbled over a couple of times, and began to cry.

The other eight contestants heard the boy cry. They slowed down and looked back. Then they all turned around and went back, every one of them. One girl with Down syndrome bent down, kissed him, and said, "This will make it better."

Then all nine linked arms and walked together to the finish line. Everyone in the stadium stood, and the cheering went on for several minutes. People who were there are still writing and telling the story.

Why? Because deep down, we know this one thing—what matters in this life is more than winning for ourselves. What truly matters in this life is helping others to win, even if it means slowing down and reaching out. Those young people heard a cry, and they acted in humility in the example of our Lord and Savior. Makes you wonder who is really disabled.

* * * * *

Sometimes we get moving too fast or forget to check something we did and some interesting things happen. Take, for instance, these real-life excerpts from people's resumes; (1) "Dear Sir, I am a rabid typist." Well, let's hope the person doesn't bite anybody. (2) "Dear Sir, I am a quick leaner." (3) "I seek challenges that test my mind and body because the two are usually not together." (4) "Here are my qualifications for you to overlook." (5) "In closing, may I say that I hope to hear from you shorty."

Given our best efforts, we sometimes make mistakes, as found in the story of the compulsive race track better who promised to attend church each Sunday with his wife if she agreed not to nag him about the nags the rest of the week. The wife agreed, hoping that this contact with religion might cure her husband of his habit.

On the very next Sunday, the couple was found seated side-by-side in the center of the church. The husband joined in singing the final hymn with such enthusiasm that several members in the nearby pews were visibly impressed.

As the couple emerged from the church, the husband acknowledged the smiles with which they were greeted, remarking in a whisper to his wife, "I'll bet you didn't expect me to make such an impression! It wouldn't surprise me if they wanted my bar room baritone in the church choir."

"You did very well, dear," his wife remarked, "except for one small thing; the word is hallelujah, not Hialeah."

* * * * *

O. Henry tells the story of love in a short story called "The Gift of the Magi." A young American couple, Della and Jim, were very poor but loved each other very much. Each one had a unique possession. Della's hair was her glory. When she let it down, it almost served as a robe. Jim had a gold watch that had come to him by his father and was his pride.

It was the day before Christmas, and Della had exactly $1.75 to buy Jim a present. She went out and sold her hair for twenty dollars and bought him a platinum chain for his watch.

When Jim came home at night and saw Della's almost shaved head, he was taken back. It was not that he did not like it or love her any less, for to him she was lovelier than ever. Slowly, he handed her his gift—it was a set of expensive tortoise-shelled combs with jeweled edges for her lovely hair. He had sold his gold watch to buy them.

Each had given the other all they had—real love cannot think of any other way to serve.

PRAYER

Dear inspiring God, You speak to my spiritual heart and mind in different ways. Sometimes through Scripture or a song or a hymn or maybe a loved one's word, but it's clear You are in that moment.

Help me look more closely for the ways You give Yourself to me in soothing times, which bring a sense of desired closeness with You.

Dear Lord, the world sometimes just tries to steal my joy; so much attention is spent on negative things that it begins to wear me down; such a false impression that only evil, hurt, and pain surround me—that life is a burden and I exist only to get from one bad day to the next. Allow Your Spirit to show me ever more clearly how I can find peace and hope in not only pleasant times but unpleasant times simply by realizing my purpose in life is to worship You in all my thoughts, words, and actions. I do not have to be thankful for all things that happen to me, but I am thankful that You are with me in all things.

You came in the life of Jesus to teach how the focus on and pursuit of material things—serving only myself and concentrating on my will and not Your will—can bring me to the place of disappointment. But by allowing Your Spirit to draw me to the teachings of Jesus and by allowing Him to be the Redeemer of my life, I am able to see more clearly the beauty in life—the beauty of the sunrise and sunset; the completeness of who I am; a deep satisfaction in the service and outreach to others who have a greater struggle; the pure joy of knowing Your presence is over and in me each day of my journey, leading me to Your eternal home, not made with human hands. Help me to strive for the excitement of life in Your name.

Guide me to challenge myself to cast off the restraints of negativism and boldly go where Your vision and will lead me. Give me eyes to see, when I walk with You, trials are not barriers, but opportunities to strengthen myself in Christian faith. Give me sufficient grace for each day, knowing joy is as simple as faith, and peace as close as trusting You and fully accepting Christ as Lord and Savior. Sing to me, in a new way, Your song of hope and peace. May my loved ones and friends feel Your soothing and comfortable presence. Also, sing to them a new song of hope and peace.

Omnipotent God, let world leaders hear more clearly Your song of peace and dignity for all Your children and let hearts be changed. These things I ask in the name of Jesus, who taught the prayer, saying, "Our Father . . ."

114

How Do You Define It?

SERMONETTE

1 John 3:11-24

There is a word that we know about because we often use it in our speech. We say, "I love your hairdo. I love your dress. I love the way my car hugs the road, etc." Other languages have different words for various aspects of "love." We use the word to mean: to like, adore, to manipulate someone, etc. *Webster's Dictionary* defines love as "passionate affection" or "to care deeply."

A woman said to her husband, "You never tell me you love me anymore."

The husband replied, "Listen, I told you when we married forty years ago that I love you. If that changes, I will let you know!"

Scripture tells us the source of our ability to love in its purest form is from God, for "God is love" (1 John 4:8). God provided the Garden of Eden and, in love, walked with Adam and Eve before they were thrown out for not obeying God's commands. Remember, being tempted is not a sin; Jesus was tempted in the wilderness. Acting on and doing the temptation is the sin. The Apostle Paul wrote in 1 Corinthians 10:13, "And God is faithful; He will not let you be tempted beyond what you can bear. But when you are tempted, He will also provide a way out so that you can endure it."

We sometimes say it another way, "When a door is shut, God opens a window." In many of his writings, Paul expressed the concept, "Bring on the temptation, for it allows me to show my love for God."

Not many of us would ask for more temptation, but resisting it is a glorious way to show love for God. Another obvious thing to remember is that satan will never tempt you to do something righteous!

Another thing I have experienced over the years is that love and hate can't live together at the same time in the same place. It's the same thing as saying light and darkness can't exist together in the same place at the same time. How do you handle temptation versus the love of God?

A husband and wife decided they would catch up on bills and not spend on clothes for three months. Two weeks later, the wife found herself passing her favorite store. She stopped and offered this prayer, "Satan, get behind me . . . and PUSH!"

Paul, in Romans 5:8, writes, "But God demonstrates His own love for us in this: While we were still sinners, Christ died for us." We want to feel and say we love God and want to be seen as loving, but what do our actions show? In other words, if you were on trial for being a Christian, would there be enough evidence to convict you?

When evilness says, "Don't get mad, get even," can you just stop at don't get mad? Can you pass the ultimate test and pray for those who persecute you? When you are put to the test (tempted), do you pass the test of passionate affection? When you say, "I love God," does that translate to *tolerate*? How about "when it's convenient" or maybe "if I don't have to pay a price."

God's love is real—can you feel it? Why or why not?

ILLUSTRATIONS

He was known as a mean, old man, resentful and bitter. Someone said that his bitterness was justified; his beloved wife died. "He has reason to be bitter," they said in town, talking about his life.

He never went to church, never had much to do with anyone. When in his late sixties, they carried him out of his apartment and over to the hospital to die, no one visited. No flowers were sent. He went there to die alone.

But there was this nurse; well, she wasn't a nurse yet, just a student nurse. She was in training, and because she was in this training, she didn't know anything that was taught about the necessity of detachment—the need for distance with a patient.

She befriended the old man. It had been so long since he had friends, he didn't know how to act with one. He told her, "Go away. Leave me alone."

She would smile and coax him to eat his Jell-O. At night she tucked the covers under the mattress. "Don't need anybody to help me," he would growl.

Soon he grew so weak, he hadn't the strength to resist her kindness. Late at night after her duties were done, she pulled up a chair and sat by his bed and sang to him in a low soft voice as she held his gnarled hand. He looked up in the dim light and just wondered. And on that night, a tear formed in his eye when she kissed him goodbye lightly on his forehead. For the first time in forty, maybe fifty years he said, "God bless you."

As she left the room now in silence, two others remained, breathless, whispering in the old man's ear the last words he heard before slipping away into the valley of death. "Thanks to her, we made it in time, and we gotcha."

The words were whispered in unison by two angels sent by Christ—one named Goodness and the other named Mercy. And in the background, the voice of the Master could be heard, "Hurry on now, for I have other sheep that are not in the fold. I must find someone to help me bring them in also so there shall be one flock and but one shepherd!"

I'm sure the young nurse-to-be had many things she could have been involved in—the world has so many exciting things to offer. But in her busy schedule, she held a stranger's hand and sang to him softly. Scriptures show us that we are not to withdraw from life but have triumphant involvement in it. When Jesus chose His twelve close disciples, He didn't choose shepherds. Shepherds were on the hillside by themselves mainly without human contact. Jesus chose fishermen, a tax collector, a physician—people who were used to the marketplace, dealing and associating with people.

We aren't to be a recluse, but be involved in life; *in* the world, but not *of* the world.

* * * * *

An old man was walking along a lone highway one cold and gray evening when he came to a chasm, vast, wide, and steep with waters rolling cold and deep. The old man crossed in the twilight dim, for the sullen stream had no fears for him. But when safe on the other side, he turned and built a bridge to span the tide.

"Old man," said a fellow pilgrim nearby, "you are wasting your strength with building here. Your journey will end with the ending day. You never again will pass this way. You've crossed the chasm, deep and wide. Why build this bridge at eventide?"

The builder lifted his old gray head. "Good friend, in the path I've been," he said, "there follows behind me a youth whose feet must pass this way. The chasm that seemed naught to me, to that fair-haired youth may a pitfall be. That youth too must cross in the twilight dim. Good friend, I am building this bridge for that youth."

Certain young persons are watching your actions. Concerning your journey in Christ, are you a chasm or a bridge?

* * * * *

When you think of your God-given gifts or talents, what comes to mind? What are the things you can do well and effortlessly, and which do you enjoy doing? If you feel you don't have a gift, you're wrong. In I Corinthians 7, the Apostle Paul lets us know that we all have at least one gift from God. The gift comes in different forms and different intensity, which makes your gift unique to you.

An elderly lady in a Methodist church was unable to participate in church activities. She felt very useless and spent time each day remembering the things she could do in the past. Then she was

118

encouraged by a friend to learn to crochet. To her surprise, she found she was good at it. In a short time, she became better and faster. She learned different patterns for afghans and was told she could sell each afghan for a very good price. She had a better idea—give them away. People in nursing homes, poor families at Christmas, newborn babies, and others received the beautiful gift of an afghan blanket. She felt a sense of pride and satisfaction in bringing joy to someone she probably would never meet.

The afghans were not for her profit, but her God-given talent was dedicated to the uplifting of others. When you pray for your gifts to be realized, look out—you may just be surprised what God, through the Holy Spirit in Jesus's name, will unveil to you.

* * * * *

An old man showed up at the back door of the house being rented by a couple. Opening the door a few inches, they saw his eyes were glassy and his furrowed face glistened with silver stubble. He clutched a wicker basket holding a few unappealing vegetables. He bid them good morning and offered his produce for sale. The couple was uneasy enough that they made a quick purchase to alleviate both their pity and their guilt and fear.

To their chagrin, he returned the next week, introducing himself as Mr. Roth, the man who lived in the shack down the road. As their fears subsided, they got close enough to realize it wasn't alcohol, but cataracts that marbleized his eyes.

On subsequent visits, he shuffled in wearing two mismatched right shoes and worn clothes. He entertained them with his harmonica. With glazed eyes set on future glory, he puffed out old gospel tunes between conversations about vegetables and religion. They got together some clothes and not wanting to embarrass him, left them on his porch.

On the next visit, he exclaimed, "The Lord is so good. I came out of my shack this morning and found a bag of shoes and clothing on my porch."

"That's wonderful, Mr. Roth," they said. "We're happy for you."

"You know what's even more wonderful?" he asked. "Just yesterday, I met some people on the other side of my shack that can use them, so this morning I left them on their porch."

We get our wants and needs mixed up many times. How do you react when you see someone who appears to be in need?

PRAYER

Dear loving God, You have traveled with me this past week through the presence of the Holy Spirit. At times, my journey has been challenging as I dealt with life issues. Some days are not as happy as other days as I try and sort out confusion over choices I have to make, disappointments over people or events, worry over payments, distraction over possible health concerns. What's it all about?

Then I come to the joy of realizing that in all things there is one thread, one anchor that I can always hold onto. My heart is drawn to the ever-present power of Your love, grace, and strength, which means I'm never alone. I'm reminded of my faith that lets me know that as we talk, or thereafter, You will provide wisdom and direction and soothe my anxiety with the understanding that this too shall pass. And as I seek answers, there may be twists and turns in Your response and my life, taking me in a direction I never would have come up with by myself. I may feel that I am on the right path, but when I encounter trials and tribulations, they just might be used by You to strengthen me to receive your blessings at a later time.

For when I take a deep breath, share my feelings and concerns with You, and, in trust, seek Your guidance and Your way, then You bless me with the peacefulness of spirit that passes worldly understanding. When I accept that You bring what I need in Your time and in Your way, then I can know what it means to "let go and let God." I will still have my role to play, but now I will wait for Your direction through prayer.

Dear God, Your presence in the life of Jesus has given me my example of righteous living. Even in His darkest hour, He prayed, "Thy will be done." So, dear God, give me a sense of Your presence to strengthen my resolve, to put aside self, and seek Your will, a real presence which will empower me to celebrate blessings You will provide for my persistent, faithful walk with You.

May I have excitement and celebration as I awake each morning with these words on my lips, "Dear God, what are we going to do today?" I lift up to You my loved ones and friends in need of Your special presence. Please bring comfort, healing, and a sense of Your closeness to each one in accordance with Your will.

In my petition to You, I continue to lift up leaders of this and other countries, that peace will reign over terror and hatred. These things I ask in the name of Jesus, who taught the prayer, saying, "Our Father . . ."

Are Stones in Your Way?

SERMONETTE

Matthew 28:1-10

A little boy came home from church all excited, "Mommy, I found out in the Easter Service that Jesus is a flower!"

"Oh," said the mother, "how do you know that?"

"Because," he replied, "we all sang, 'Jesus a rose, Jesus a rose.'"

From the first day of His life, Jesus was destined for Jerusalem and crucifixion. And after three years of ministry, the religious leaders decided he had to go, now. He was speaking of the way to the heavenly Kingdom, bringing relief to the poor, healing the sick, and preaching to the "haves" about their arrogance, pride, and selfishness. He had to go! There was no room in their world for one who taught (1) You are your brother's keeper, (2) Worship no idol (possessions, money, etc.)—only God, and (3) We are saved by faith, not works (however, your faith or lack of faith can be seen in your works, deeds, and actions).

But above all, we understand that in the Good Friday event (death of Jesus), He died that all our sins can be forgiven. You haven't done anything which God won't forgive when you bring it to God with a truly repentant heart. "For God so loved the world that He gave His one and only Son, that whoever believes in Him shall not perish but have eternal life" (John 3:16).

In Mark 16:1-20, we find one of the gospel accounts of the resurrection. Mark explains how certain women brought spices to prepare the body, and they wondered who was going to roll away the stone at the entrance to the tomb. They and many others thought Jesus was still there. If He had been there, our faith would have been finished. The gospel writers would have written, "They killed Jesus and put Him in a tomb—period!"

But they found the tomb empty. God had reached down and taken Jesus home! One of the greatest lessons found over and over in Scripture—when it looks the worst, you can't count God out! But these women expected to see the worst—a dead Jesus. Because the tomb was empty, we relish in the hope of one day joining Him.

Let's talk about that stone. It was heavy, covered the entrance, and was sealed to protect the darkness, decay, and foul air from escaping. A trench was usually dug at the front of the entrance, which the large stone sat in. The women were justifiably concerned about who would help them remove this impediment to their work. However, when the women came, it had already been removed (not so Jesus could get out!), and the angel was there who told them, "He is not here."

Sometimes we have stones in our spiritual hearts—prejudice, pride, or not caring for the plight of others. I have noticed over the years that God is in the business of rolling away stones. Also, the closer you walk with Christ, the fewer number of stones there are to roll away, stones that keep us from complete and true belief and even affect our resurrection to a heavenly home. Stones are so heavy and many times are too heavy for us alone to move, but God can.

Let go of the stones big and small which are blocking your spiritual heart, and let God remove them. The process is all set up. The actors are in place and ready to act. Are you?

ILLUSTRATIONS

On the fourth Thursday of November, people gather around many tables to celebrate a day of thanksgiving. I once heard of a four-year-old who was asked to return thanks before just such a dinner. The family members bowed their heads in expectation and waited . . . and waited.

After a long silence, the young fellow looked up at his mother and asked, "But if I thank God for the broccoli, won't He know that I'm lying?"

And then the story of a family entertaining guests for dinner on a freezing Thanksgiving Day. When all were seated, the man of the house turned to his six-year-old and asked her to say grace.

"But, Daddy, I don't know what to say," she protested.

"Oh, just say what you've heard me say," the mother chimed in.

Obediently, she bowed her little head and said, "Oh, Lord, why did you let me invite these people I don't even like here on such a cold day? Amen."

The last prayer you shared with God—when did you say that was? Were you honest? Did you want God's hand in your affairs or were you just trying to hedge your bets, just in case? I believe we sometimes actually feel we can fool God; then there's the moment of truth when God reveals to us our true motives. How about right now? Can you have an honest prayer with God? Honestly tell God how you feel and seek to feel His ever presence. Then you can feel a sense of expectation as you wait for the blessing. But be ready and don't be surprised because the intervention might come in ways you weren't expecting!

* * * * *

Sin; somebody is hurt. Somebody who deserves to be loved is denied love. Sin, which means breaking away from God, is a three-letter word with the letter "I" right in the middle. The devil paints such a pretty picture, but his way is destruction. He paints it with such pretty colors that it seems the way is good for us.

Only later do we see it for what it is and realize that prayer would have made it clear for what it was. So, we are faced with the question—why don't we pray over decisions before we make them?

* * * * *

Evangelist Billy Graham visited American soldiers in Korea during the time of hostilities there. He made it a point to go to the hospitals and talk and pray with those who had been wounded.

One day as he was visiting a hospital, he met a young man who was lying face down in a canvas cradle because his spine had been shattered by a bullet. A hole had been cut in the bottom of the cradle so the soldier could see through to the floor. While Reverend Graham was talking to him, the young soldier said, "I wish I could see your face, Reverend Graham, so I could see what you look like."

Billy Graham got down on his back and worked his way under the cradle so the young man could look down at his face.

Is this not a crude analogy of what God has done in Jesus Christ? God came down to our level so that humans would see what God is like. The next time you hesitate going to God in prayer because He won't understand, reflect on the fact that He came to experience our joys, fears, pain, and hurt. He understands!

* * * * *

After Judas hanged himself, the disciples wanted to fill the "position." So, they put forth the names of Joseph and a man named Matthias. The names were put on many pieces of paper separately and put in a container with an open neck. The container was shaken vigorously until one of the names was "cast out" of the jar. This, they felt, was God's way of picking the man He wanted.

And does anybody know which man God picked? Matthias is correct. And so, Matthias became a substitute for Judas. I have a story about substitution that I want to tell because it will lead us into Scripture.

Cliff Barrows, song leader for the Billy Graham Crusade ministry, told the story about his children when they were younger. They had done something that he had forbidden them to do. They had been told that if they did the same thing again, they would be disciplined. When he returned home from work, again they hadn't minded, but his heart went out to them. "I just could not discipline them," he said. He continued, "Bobby and Bettie Ruth were very small. I called them into my room, took off my belt, and then my shirt. With a bare back, I knelt at the bed. I made them strap me with the belt ten times each; you should have heard the crying. From them, I mean; the crying was from them.

They didn't want to do it, but I told them the penalty had to be paid and through their sobs and tears, they completed the job. I smile when I remember that incident," he continued. "I must admit I wasn't much of a hero. It hurt. I haven't offered to do that again. It was a once-for-all sacrifice. But I never had to spank those two children again because they got the point. We kissed each other and when it was over, we prayed together. I don't understand how it happened, but there seemed to be a presence leading me that day."

There was one occasion where the price was paid for us. How many of us really "get the point?" We aren't able to be perfect or reach a magic quota of good works to save our souls. The Perfect One took the lashings and paid the ultimate price for our salvation. But we must participate in our redemption by living the Christian life.

The New Testament Book of James tells us we are known by how we act, not by what we say. Did your actions today and will your actions tomorrow demonstrate to the world that you "get it?"

* * * * *

"Hey, Father," said a man talking to a priest. "You got it all wrong about this prayer and God stuff. He doesn't exist. I ought to know."

"Why's that, my son?" asked the priest.

"Well," the man said, "when I was ice fishing in the Arctic far from the nearest village, a blizzard blew up with wind and blinding snow. I was a goner. So, I got down on my knees and prayed real hard, begging God for help."

"And did He help you?"

"Heck, no," said the man. "God didn't lift a finger. Some Eskimo appeared out of nowhere and showed me the way."

When you pray for something and it happens, is that just luck?

* * * * *

In the shipwreck scene of *The Tempest*, the mariners speak for the whole company when they say, "All is lost; to prayers, to prayers!"

For this forgotten group of sailors and many others, prayer was not something to live with daily, but to die with. Religion was the last resort. When you reach a dead-end, try prayer. But that's all right, Scripture teaches us it's better late than never. However, think of the spiritual anguish which could be saved if Jesus was involved through prayer at the very beginning of our process before decisions were made.

PRAYER

Everlasting and Benevolent God, I pause on my earthly journey to praise and worship You. I ask for forgiveness where I have not been obedient to Your will and where I have put self over others, worldly pursuits, and activities instead of light for my path from my Savior, Jesus the Christ. Let Your Holy Spirit direct me closer to Your ways in days to come.

Heavenly God, as I lift up those in the church who have searched their hearts and have accepted leadership and support roles of ministry, I pray courage, wisdom, compassion, and love will be among the many gifts given to them. Through their influence, dear God, help me to reach for new visions of Your will and be open to challenges of service and embolden me to seek ways, old and new, to reach out to make disciples of Jesus.

As I decide to witness to You and my faith and trust, show me the way for increased service and increased harvest. Enable me to grow more spiritual in prayer and daily living. Excite me about the possibilities that await, but only in trust.

I am also aware that many of Your children now find life challenging. Strengthen their resolve to remain faithful, even in times of trial. As is Your will, use me to take Your message of peace, comfort, and hope to those who suffer in mind, body, or spirit. May all of us who call ourselves Christian be guided to the least, the lost, and the lonely.

Loving God, as many are ravaged by the effects of disease, war, and terror, persuade world leaders to tire of such things and seek the betterment of all Your children. These things I ask in the name of Jesus, the Risen Savior, who taught the prayer, saying, "Our Father . . ."

Which Level Are You On?

SERMONETTE

Matthew 21:1-11

The first four gospel writers of the New Testament all talked about Jesus's triumphal entry into Jerusalem. It's significant that Jesus rode into town on a donkey which, at the time, was a symbol of peace. There was a very large crowd, as most of the people had seen Him in places like Galilee where He performed miracles. But here they cried out "Hosanna" (save us, we pray), spread their tunics on the ground, and when they saw Him riding a lowly donkey, they went home to their usual ways! Why not ride a black stallion—a sign of strength? They sized Him up very quickly; He wasn't what they wanted.

How and when did Jesus ride into your life? Are you just standing in the crowd at a distance, or have you gotten up close and personal? Do you *know* Him or just *about* Him? Even the devil knows about Him but doesn't accept Him as Lord and Savior.

When He traveled to the door of your heart, did you tell Him there were certain places He couldn't go, such as the place you store racist thoughts, hate for people who don't look like you, etc.? I believe we have three basic responses when we are aware of Jesus's calling to triumphantly enter our life.

(1) He is accepted as Lord of my life. There are no significant decisions without asking, "What would Jesus do?" You don't have to ask Him things such as, "Is it all right to comb my hair ?" Just as in Texas hold 'em, we are 100 percent all-in.

(2) We invite Him into certain parts of our life. We don't want Jesus in those parts of our life where He could cause trouble or conflict over things we want to do, feel, or believe. Here we are about 45-50 percent in.

(3) Jesus, I'm not ready at this time for a commitment. I will talk the talk but not walk the walk.

A bold believer was lecturing on the folly of religion, especially Christianity, and at the end, he asked for questions. A young man who was eating an apple stood up and as he took another bite, asked the lecturer, "Was this apple sweet or sour?"

"That's ridiculous," the lecturer said. "I haven't tasted it. How could I know?"

"Exactly," said the student. "You haven't spiritually tasted the presence of Christ; how would you know?"

There's a famous painting of Jesus knocking on the subtle impression of a person's heart. Upon close examination, one notices the doorknob is on the inside and the caption reads, "Will you let Him in?"

The decision to accept Jesus into your life and to live with Christlike behavior should not be made lightly. If you made that decision, what level are you living in? I don't know any place in the Bible where Jesus said, "Believe halfway in me." Do you?

ILLUSTRATIONS

. . . that's the way it was with disciples of Jesus. He was their life, their identity, and their hope. There is an eighty-foot-tall maple tree in Milford, Connecticut, that hasn't changed much over the years. There are new leaves every spring, of course, and the leaves fall off every autumn. And there's a spot where a limb came off when hurricane Gloria blew through in 1985. Other than that missing branch, the tree on Hausley Avenue has looked the same for as long as anyone can remember.

However, the spot where the limb was blown off caused quite a stir in the neighborhood some time back. One of the residents looked at the tree one day and saw what looked like the face of

Jesus. "It took my breath away," she recalled. "I told my friend to come over and pretty soon we had the entire neighborhood here looking at it."

Word spread quickly throughout the area, and before anyone realized it, the maple tree became a popular attraction as car after car drove by to see the face of Jesus on the tree where the limb broke from the tree. The lady who first made the discovery described herself as someone who attended church but was not overly religious—whatever that means. She told a reporter, "I'm not reading the Bible all the time."

The tree for her was some sort of sign though. "I just think people may be able to take some hope from it," she said.

Another neighbor took her seventeen-year-old son to touch the tree in hope that it would cure him of seizures that he suffers. "You never know," she said.

Another resident said she took her three children to see the tree. "We have a lot of single mothers in the neighborhood and teenagers who have to make tough decisions in these times." She saw the face in the tree as a message of hope. She said it was like a message to have faith in ourselves and to have hope for the world.

The residents of Milford saw what looked like the face of Jesus on an old tree. In recent years, people have reported seeing Christ's face on the side of a barn and on a town's water tower, among other places.

Where do we find Jesus? We find Him in the pages of our Bible and in places we least expect. Dr. Tom Troeger recalls the time he had to be away from his home and fiancee. As he sat in a small bus station feeling depressed, he looked up, and an elderly woman was sitting across from him at the U-shaped counter. The woman said, "You sure do look down and depressed."

Troeger replied, "I am down and depressed."

And for an uncontrollable reason, he started to cry. He told the woman his story. The woman told him she had been married to a traveling salesman who had since passed away. They used to weep every time her husband had to go away. Nevertheless, they were happy each time they came together. "You're going to have a wonderful marriage. Everything will be fine for you."

She suggested he might feel better if he ate something and ordered a huge slice of freshly baked bread. "Eat this," as with delicate hands she broke the bread in half and placed it before him.

Just then an announcement came over the speakers, and the woman cried, "That's my bus." She got up and left.

"Just then my teary eyes opened," Troeger concluded. "And I recognized that Christ was being shown to me by the action of that woman."

Where will you meet the Risen Christ this day, this week, and will you recognize Him? And would you be willing to pray that you are given the opportunity for someone to be drawn to Christ through your words, action, or witness? Think about yesterday; did you reflect the living Christ?

* * * * *

Hope can often be found, or maybe not, due to the actions of people. In 1942, a man named Felix Powell sat down at a piano to play an old tune. He had every right to play it; he had written it himself. It had been tremendously popular in both World Wars. He was singing it now, "So pack up your troubles in your old kit bag and smile, smile, smile."

When Felix Powell finished his song, he walked into his bedroom, took out a revolver, put it to his head, and shot himself. Although some admitted that they felt he was quieter lately than usual, no one reached out to Felix, and no hope was found. We first must realize that when we talk uplifting things to people, we could be the very ones who gave them hope. But when we talk hurtful, negative things about that person or when we fail to uplift them, we could be the very one who takes away their hope.

Our silence, failure to act, or acting in a hurtful way could keep them from seeing that glimmer of hope. Can you find a passage in the Scripture where Jesus spoke negatively about someone instead of lifting them up? Just a kind word for that woman in line at the grocery store could be the very words she needs to find hope.

* * * * *

In a medium-sized church in a large Southern town, a parishioner by the name of Thomas was known to almost everyone. When Thomas died, the pastor noticed that at the funeral, a soldier who he didn't recognize, came to the casket and gave old Thomas a salute fit for a king. Following the service, the pastor walked with the soldier, who was nothing less than a brigadier general.

The soldier said, "Pastor, you're probably wondering what I'm doing here. Years ago, Thomas was my Sunday school teacher. I was a wild lad, and he never knew what he did for me with his gentle, constructive ways. I owe everything I am or will be to him. Today I had to salute him at this end time."

Thomas didn't know that what he was doing, in all probability, was changing lives. He only wanted to be fertile soil for the love of Jesus Christ so he could share this with others and encourage them. It's my desire and hope that each of us individually and as a body of Christians will experience spiritual satisfaction like never before as we become even better soil for the joys and challenges which Christ will bring.

How about you today? How does that desire and hope sound to you?

* * * * *

As we talk about hope, you might have heard the story about the long and rough Atlantic crossing where the seasick passenger was leaning over the rail of the ocean liner and had turned several shades of green. A steward came along and tried to cheer him up by saying, "Don't be discouraged, sir! You know, no one's ever died of seasickness yet!"

The nauseous passenger looked up at the steward with sorrow-filled eyes and said, "Oh, don't say that! It's only the hope of dying that kept me alive long enough to get to the railing!"

Hope—the feeling that something we want to happen will happen, and we don't have anything to prove it with. Without any evidence, we still believe it will happen. In the midst of our confusing life, we still have hope; we believe that peace is possible. For through the biblical stories, we see that when people thought all was lost, Jesus shows up and gives them the message, "Cast that burden on me."

We then know that Jesus can defeat that which is holding us down. Hope is realized and a new day begins. But don't just hope—couple that hope with a strong walk with the Risen Christ. Hope alive with Jesus is an awareness of our future. Realistic hope and the presence of Christ—now there's something to get excited about!

* * * * *

There were times when there was a disconnect between what Jesus was saying and what people heard. Even the disciples were confused over phrases such as "born again," and sometimes He would speak of exciting things and then tell them not to tell anyone else.

In John 4:13-15, Jesus promises a Samaritan woman water to drink so she would never be thirsty again. You can imagine her surprise and her desire to get this water so she wouldn't have to come to the well every day.

Sometimes in your relationship with Jesus, you have to dig a little deeper to uncover the true advice or answer to prayer. It's comparable to the riddle of the windmill that was five stories high and had five corners on each floor, including the ground floor. The windmill owner and his wife stood on one corner and two cats stood in each of the other corners. How many feet are on the windmill? (Answer below.)

It's also important to note that when a person goes to a well to draw water, they don't carry buckets filled with water. They take empty buckets. When you go to the life-giving well, all idols of worship must be left behind—love of money, desire for prestige, power over people, etc. The belief that Jesus lived, then died on the cross for our salvation, was risen from the dead, and now is alive must be the form of your empty bucket. And when Jesus, as Living Water, comes into your life, you will never be the same. Feeling spiritually empty? There are buckets of living water available just for the asking. Why not come to the well and drink?

(Answer to the riddle—four, the owner and his wife. Cats have paws.)

PRAYER

Heavenly God, as I entered this calendar year, I struggled with issues left over from the previous year, and I am still dealing with them now. There was a newness and freshness over the start of this year, but I have a sense of unsettlement, confusion, hurt, as well as a sense of betrayal over certain incidents in my life that didn't go away with the turn of a calendar page. I long to move forward and bring resolution to these matters, but I still can't let go and grant forgiveness or stop searching for the answer to the question why.

But even in this condition in my life, I know that peace can be mine if I can but let go, turn the matter over to You, and move on. In this and other unpleasant things, I sometimes feel the dark force trying to hold me back. You gave me the gifts of Jesus and the Holy Spirit to journey with me each day of my life and Your continued presence of wisdom, yet I seem to be stuck. I know the world will continue to bring some unpleasant things and I am not alone. The larger picture for the journey is that I am on my way to the eternal home, and *still,* I try and solve this hindrance by myself.

Dear Lord, I confess that many times I am the victim of my own decisions, whether by action or inaction, times like when I haven't sufficiently talked a situation over with You or maybe with someone of wisdom You have placed in my path. There are more than likely new situations that will startle me because of the possible effect on my life. But You have promised that nothing, except me, can separate me from Your great love; that Your grace, strength, and uplifting presence is all I need. That in all things, You are near, preparing a better day for those who believe and trust in You.

Help my faith to grow and allow me to find Your path in resolving all things which bother me. Maybe in Your will, I will have to do the hard thing—apologize, admit I was wrong, say I overreacted—but show me the way to a peaceful solution. Let me have a search for truth, not pride. In my spiritual journey, I truly don't know what's around the corner, only that You go with me and I need to consult with You all the time.

So on this day, I pray for release from my concerns, that my heart will be joyful knowing that in all things You want to be my partner and give me the strength to endure, wisdom to be guided, peace as I trust, and victory for my faithfulness.

I ask these things in the name of Jesus, who taught the prayer, saying, "Our Father . . ."

What Does It Take for You to Break Free?

SERMONETTE

Luke 12:4-7

One of the obstacles that keep us from being all that we can be, given our God-given talents to achieve, is fear. Fear is defined as anxiety caused by real or assumed situations. These are things we view as potentially harmful to us. If you see a tornado coming toward you, there would be real danger. On the other hand, it would be hard to comprehend if someone said, "I just won one million dollars, and I'm so fearful!"

A lot of people have a fear of failure. Maybe you have an unhealthy attitude toward fear. Maybe you grew up in a family where a price was paid for any mistake; penalties were given in the form of judgmental actions, scolding (emotional abuse leaves long-lasting scars), or withholding love while the bar of acceptance was so high it could never have been reached. And if by some miracle you did approach success, guess what? The bar is moved higher!

You bring these rules, regulations, shoulds, and oughts, as well as new ones, with you into adulthood. Why try something new when we don't have the confidence to succeed and know, when we fail, there's going to be a huge price to pay? So, we learn not to take a risk unless we are absolutely sure we can succeed, and even then, it's hard to do.

The word "risk-taker" does not belong in such situations. We have allowed ourselves to be placed in a sort of prison, and we decide to stay there. We don't want to go through the painful exercise of deciding who chose this path of fear for us and discovering the methods they use to limit our emotional, mental, and spiritual growth.

I have seen people still controlled by a mom or dad who died ten years before. We settle for our families' fears when God has so much more in store for us. God didn't make you to always be perfect—you can strive for it, but don't beat yourself up if you don't make it! When you tackle your fears, you might make mistakes, but tackling your fears may be the way you learn that fear has robbed you of so many good experiences.

I had a former student tell me about a wonderful trip he had taken from his Virginia home to Florida. Knowing he was fearful of flying, I asked him how long it took to make the drive.

He answered, "I finally overcame my fear and took an airplane. It was such a great experience; I regret that for years I could have been flying and enjoying things, but I was just too darn afraid."

Fear can rob you of so many blessings. Maybe you would like to visit in the nursing homes (can't—might not know what to say), sing in the choir (can't—might miss a note), visit families (can't—might intrude). Psychologists tell us 95 percent of fears in your head are "paper tigers" and have nothing to do with reality.

Are you tired of making up excuses to satisfy your fears? Evil wants to hold you in bondage, but God wants to liberate you to become fully the person you were intended to be. What fear holds you back? There are 365 "Fear nots" in the Bible; one for each day.

Take your fear to God in prayer; pray for the Holy Spirit to guide you. And for heaven's sake, when the answer comes, be bold! Take a risk! I promise you, the world will not end!

In Psalm 23:4, we find these words, "Even though I walk through the darkest valley, I will fear no evil, for you are with me."

You might make a mistake trying something new, but you might make a greater mistake *not* trying something new! You don't wear literal handcuffs; why put on figurative ones?

As far as making mistakes go, in my first appointment, I thought I had done well preparing the worship format for the Sunday service. But as I was preparing to end the service on the second Sunday, I heard the organist say in a low voice, "Preacher, if you expect to get paid, you had better start taking up an offering!"

With such a mistake, I guess I could have quit the ministry! I chose to share it with the congregation; we all had a good laugh. Adopt an attitude that some of your greatest learning lessons will come from mistakes. The question for today is, since you are going to make mistakes, what are you going to do with them?

ILLUSTRATIONS

In a small coal-mining town of Kentucky, Grandma Richardson was admired by everyone in town for her courage and unwavering faith. She had buried a husband and one son killed in the mine. Then it happened again. Another son was killed in the mine. After the funeral, one of the children of the town saw her sitting on the porch and asked, "Grandma Richardson, aren't you sad today?"

"Yes," she replied. "I am sad, very sad. It's hard to say goodbye to someone you love, and I have had to do it three times. But," she told the child, "I have something more than sadness inside of me." She then spoke of her faith.

"Can you give me some?" the child asked.

"Why, child," Grandma Richardson answered, "I have been giving it to you for years now. It's knowing that God loves you and He makes one promise that is a gift—the most valuable gift in the world. God promised that no matter what happens to us, no matter how good or bad things may be, regardless of your joy or sorrow, God will not leave you alone."

That is God's promise to each of us. It goes part and parcel with our baptism. To understand baptism is to become a new person. It's God who has saved us through the sacrifice of Christ. It's God who calls us into a new life of service. It's God who goes with us and will one day welcome us to our heavenly home. What good news!

* * * * *

A woman and her grandmother—a very forgiving and religious soul—were sitting on their porch discussing a member of the family. "He's just no good," the young woman said. "He's completely untrustworthy, not to mention lazy."

"Yes, he's bad," the grandmother said as she rocked back and forth in her rocker. "But Jesus loves him."

"I'm not so sure of that," the younger woman persisted.

"Oh, yes," assured the elderly lady. "Jesus loves him." She rocked and thought for a few minutes and then added, "Of course, Jesus doesn't know him like we do!"

* * * * *

A rich man named Carl loved to ride his horse through his vast estate to congratulate himself on his wealth. One day on such a ride, he came upon Hans, an old tenant farmer who had sat down to eat his lunch in the shade of a great oak tree. Hans's head was bowed in prayer. When Hans looked up, he said, "Oh excuse me, sir. I didn't see you. I was giving thanks for my food."

"Humph," snorted the rich man Carl. He noticed the coarse dark bread and cheese which made up the old man's lunch. "If that were all I had to eat, I don't think I would feel like giving thanks."

"Oh," replied Hans. "It's quite sufficient. But it's remarkable that you should come by today. Sir, I feel I should tell you I had a strong dream just before awakening this morning."

"And what did you dream?" Carl asked with an amused smile.

The old man answered, "There was beauty and peace all around, and yet I could hear a voice saying, 'The richest man in the valley will die tonight.'"

"Dreams," cried Carl. "Nonsense." He turned and galloped away.

Hans prayed as he watched horse and rider disappear.

Die tonight, mused Carl. *It was ridiculous*. He tried to forget it, but he couldn't. But now he didn't feel too well. That evening he went to see his doctor, and he shared the old man's dream—how the richest man in the valley would die that night.

"Sounds like poppycock to me" And after an examination, he said, "Carl, you're as strong and as healthy as that horse of yours. There's no way you are going to die tonight."

Carl thanked the doctor and told him how foolish he felt at being upset by the old man's dream.

It was about 9:00 a.m. when a messenger arrived at Carl's door. "It's old Hans," the messenger said. "He died last night in his sleep."

Does the love of God let you know what it is to be truly rich?

* * * * *

A man was trying to read a serious book, but his little son kept interrupting him. He leaned against his knees and said, "Daddy, I love you!"

The father patted him and said rather absently, "Yes, son. I love you too," and he gave the boy a little push away so he could keep on reading.

But that didn't satisfy the boy, and he ran to his father and said, "I love you, Daddy," as he jumped up on his lap and threw his arms around him and gave him a hug and a squeeze, explaining, "and I've just got to do something about it."

As we grow in love, we aren't content with small-talk, pat-on-the-head love; be a nice husband now, let me finish this; be a nice wife now, don't bother me; be a nice neighbor now, stay on your side of the fence.

No, when we walk in love, we want to get involved and do something about it. What is love leading you to do today?

* * * * *

The story is told of a man who never opened the car door for his wife or any other woman. He felt it was a sissy thing to do, certainly not the macho thing to do. "Besides," he was fond of saying, "she doesn't have two broken arms."

After many years of marriage, the wife died, and her husband was heartbroken, for he truly did love her. Somehow, as the pallbearers brought her casket out of the funeral service, the husband and his family reached the hearse ahead of them. The mortician was back a few feet, and since he knew the husband quite well, he called him by name and said, "Bob, help us out. Open the door for her, will you?"

The man reached for the door handle and then for several seconds just froze. He realized he had never opened a car door for her in life. Now in her death, it would be the first, last, and only time. It was a moment for him when years of regrets came crashing down around him.

Don't put off the little things for loved ones; you might not get another chance.

PRAYER

And now, Most Ever-present God, I bow in humble adoration as I rejoice in Your presence with me. May I first reflect on any of my actions or inactions which weren't found to be pleasing to You these past days. I get caught up in my worldly activities and pursuits and forget to talk to You about Your will. I hear the inner voice Your Spirit brings and yet allow fear or indifference to reduce my spiritual efforts.

There are times when I am aware of Your request upon me but fear the consequences of getting out of my comfort zone, times when I feel the opportunity to reach out with an invitation to worship service or give testimony to the peace I find in Christ the Risen Savior, yet the darkness around me tends to silence my voice.

Create in me a new heart, O God. Let me rise to new and expanded ways in Your name. Open my heart to encourage more prayerful talks with You. Guide me as to how I can walk in faith, not fear. Keep in my being the understanding that, in all things, You work for the good.

Dear God, allow the Holy Spirit, who is ever-present, to excite me, to challenge me, to convict my desires in order to excel in service to You and not to just marginally "get by." Let me not rise or fall on my own efforts but by faith and trust in Your great intercessions that will make the way straight and give me the victory. Over and over in Scripture, I see Your great work in many of Your children who are set apart by the magnitude of their faith. Embolden me to see that great things can happen to me when I walk in great faith.

Gracious God, allow Your Spirit to comfort, heal, and bring peace to those I name in my heart. Let their faith increase and draw them closer to You. May faith bind together the hearts and resolve of righteous people everywhere to stand against evil terror and atrocities.

These I pray to You in love, confidence, and faith using the words of our Lord and Savior who taught the prayer saying, "Our Father . . ."

What to Do When You Get Nothing or No

Titus 3:3-8

Let's say you find a $100 bill on the street, and there is no one around. Do you praise God or is it just luck?

A man was on a diet and went by a donut shop. As he got close to the shop, he prayed, "God, if I am to buy donuts, please find me a close parking space." After nineteen times around the block, there it was—right in front of the shop!

Are these the will of God? Sometimes when we pray for guidance, we get a no or a yes, but there are also times when we get silence. In Luke 22:39, Jesus prayed at the Mount of Olives, "Father, if You are willing, take this cup from me; yet not my will, but Yours be done" (crucifixion).

Jesus got a no. It was the Father's will that all God's children have salvation offered to them. Jesus handled this by these words: "Not my will but Yours be done."

There are times when God's no seems to say, "I desire that you go through this, experience it, and learn from it. You will need this to receive what is coming."

When God presents a blessing, many times there are twists and turns in the journey before you get there. It is during these *no* or silent times that we should maintain a strong conviction and not give up on God because we don't get our way. Instead of seeing this as preparation, the evil of the world wants you to feel discouraged and encourages you to lose faith. But faith allows us to say, "I might be down now, but you just wait and see what God, through the Holy Spirit, does with it!"

By trusting God, we have the assurance that we won't have a burden greater than the strength we will be given by God to handle that situation (1 Corinthians 10:13). Strength does not see *no* as a defeat but as an opportunity. Remember, in 1 Thessalonians 5:18, Paul writes, "Give thanks *in* all circumstances; for this is God's will *for* you in Christ Jesus."

Give thanks *in* all circumstances, not *for;* when your car breaks down, you don't have to give thanks that it broke down (for), but we do give thanks that even *in* this, God will give wisdom, strength, and guidance through the Holy Spirit.

Also, make sure you aren't praying a selfish prayer.

A husband and wife, both sixty years old, were visited by an angel of the Lord. They were told that each could have one wish granted. The wife wished for travel. *Poof*—she had tickets in her hand.

The man said, "I wish for a wife thirty years younger than me." *Poof*—he was now ninety years old!

When you get a no, be patient and continue to praise God. Let God turn the no to yes in God's way and God's time. It's okay to ask, but remember to say, "Thy will be done," because God might have a totally different idea far better than what you were going for.

Can your faith survive no answer or a "no" answer?

ILLUSTRATIONS

A man was vacationing in Savannah, Georgia. One day while swimming, a huge wave hit him, and the undertow kept him down. He couldn't get up and thought he was going to die. The short of the story is that he was rescued and says it is the best thing that ever happened to him. It changed his life. It changed his values, his commitments, and his priorities. It drew him closer to his family. It changed his attitude about God—he became closer to God. "I wish the wave had hit me thirty years ago," he says.

In the California earthquake, a man who was able to escape a burning vehicle gave testimony of how this brought him closer to finding God's purpose in his life. We give God praise and thanks for both endings, but the question remains, just like with Jonah, why do we wait for the catastrophe to find out what God wants us to do? To find out what a genuine closeness to Christ feels like? All of us should know, by prayer and Scripture reading, God will make His purpose known.

We know Christ's great commission to go and make disciples by not only what we say but, more importantly, how we act. We are all acquainted with the parable of the Good Samaritan. We know we should be reaching out to others, and that could very well mean people not necessarily like us. We know these things; they are written in our Bible. Many times, we are in our comfort zone and just don't want to hear what God has to ask.

When we leave, will the world be a better place because we lived? Why wait for the catastrophe to fully enjoy life, shower love on those close to you, and step out boldly for service to others in Christ's name? How would you change your life if you knew positively that you had only several months to live? Why wait for the catastrophe? Why not live life to the fullest now, dedicated to and based on Jesus? What is your rationalization?

* * * * *

Lent is a time to bring order where there is chaos in our life. It's a time to reflect on our walk with God. It's time to improve our relationship with God.

A young soldier who was fighting in Italy during World War II jumped into a foxhole just ahead of some bullets. He immediately tried to deepen the hole for more protection and was frantically scraping away the dirt with his hands. He unearthed something metal and brought up a silver crucifix, a cross, left by a former resident of the foxhole.

A moment later, another leaping figure landed beside him as the shells screamed overhead. When the soldier got a chance to look, he saw that his new companion was an army chaplain. Holding out the cross, the soldier gasped, "Am I glad to see you! How do you work this thing?"

Lent is a time of reflection, a time to enter the desert alone with God and to learn how to "use this thing."

* * * * *

Disciples we are called to be,
Whose eyes are opened wide to see
The ministry that Jesus taught,
As one we share in deed and thought.

The speck we find in neighbor's eyes
May hide the log that in us lies.
We cannot help another know
If we ourselves refuse to grow.

To bear good fruit, we must rely
On God, who will identify
Within our hearts, the good that's there
And give to us abundant care.

Whoever hears and does not do,
Is blocking God from breaking through
Into our lives, as day by day
We seek to build by Jesus's way.

* * * * *

I recently heard about a man who awoke one morning to find a puddle of water in the middle of his king-size waterbed. To fix the puncture, he rolled the heavy mattress outdoors and filled it once again with water so he could locate the leak more easily.

The enormous bag of water was impossible to control, and it began rolling on the hilly terrain. He tried to hold it back, but it headed downhill and landed in a clump of bushes, which poked it full of holes.

Disgusted, he threw out the waterbed frame and moved a standard bed into the room. The next morning, he awoke to find a puddle of water in the middle of the new bed. Then he discovered that the upstairs bathroom had a leaky drain.

Christian or not, there are surprises!

* * * * *

Mrs. Rosenberg, a Jewish lady, was stranded one night late in a fashionable resort in Cape Cod—one that did not admit Jews. The desk clerk told her, "No room, the hotel is full."

The Jewish lady said, "But the sign reads vacancies."

The clerk stammered, "We don't admit Jews."

She stiffened and said, "But I converted to your religion!"

The desk clerk said, "Oh, yeah? How was Jesus born?"

"To a virgin in a manger in Bethlehem."

"That's right," said the clerk. "And why was he born in a manger?"

Mrs. Rosenberg said loudly, "Because a jerk like you in the hotel wouldn't give a Jewish lady a room!"

Was she correct?

* * * * *

I believe too many Christians today approach faith like the little boy whose mother asked him to go to the cellar and get her a can of tomato soup. The little boy didn't want to go down in the cellar alone, and he said, "Mommy, it's dark in there, and I am afraid."

"It's alright, Johnny," she said. "You go down there and get a can of tomato soup. I need it now for a recipe."

He said, "But, Mommy, it's dark, and I'm scared to go in there by myself."

"It's okay, Johnny," she said again. "Jesus will be in there with you. Now you go and get a can of tomato soup."

Johnny went to the door and opened it slowly. When he peeked inside, it was dark, and he was scared. His hands began to tremble, but he got an idea. He said in a loud voice, "Jesus, if you're down there, would you please hand me that can of tomato soup?"

Is our faith strong enough, or do we say *if* Jesus can hear and help us? Do we pray to God asking *can* God help us? Or, following prayer, do you know that help is on the way? Which way do you pray?

PRAYER

Dear God, You are the Architect and Creator of all things good. As Your child, I am free to accept the presence of Your love or to reject it. The peace found in trust and faith in You, the assurance of hope now and in the Kingdom provided for my very soul is mine for the taking. Your presence in the Holy Spirit to counsel, comfort, and lead is always available to me. Yet during my earthly journey, I am often distracted by the lies and false promises of the dark spirit. There are even times when I am lured into actual behavior which sets me apart from Your will.

When I omit prayer and scriptural preparation, I allow myself to be separated from Your great love. I let the world influence me to trade love for hate, peace of mind and spirit for confusion and anxiety, hope for despair, and trust and faith for a consuming need to make decisions without Your counsel. In the name of Jesus, please accept my plea for forgiveness and instill within me a desire for a right relationship with You. Dear God, help me to fully comprehend that I am on a journey and this is not my final resting place. Let me in my free will decide to cherish more my relationship with You, which will lead me to become more Christlike.

Let me seek ways to use my gifts and talents received from You to uplift others, to serve, and even to lead others to accept

Christ by the way I live my life and by my testimony of love and acceptance of Christ as my Lord and Savior.

Dear God of Truth, in the gifts and talents You have given me, there is at least one that will lead me to a joyful understanding of my purpose in life, a uniqueness about each of Your children which fits into Your overall design. Give me the confidence to seek that path in Your name, to pursue it with enthusiasm, and to join my heart in love with You as I fulfill my journey in Your name.

For those in trials, give them the assurance of Your love and peace of Your presence and in Your will the healing desired. May Your love find its way into the hearts of those who are in leadership roles. These things I pray in the precious name of Jesus who taught the prayer saying, "Our Father . . ."

What Would Your Neighbor Say?

SERMONETTE

John 21:1-14

Have you ever attended a class reunion only to discover that you recognize only a few people who were former classmates? Some you might have recognized by their voice or certain body movements, but as to the others, you had no clue. Then the question becomes, did they recognize you? How would you describe yourself then as compared to now? Certainly, there are physical changes, but how about changes not seen on the outside?

For instance, have you always considered yourself a Christian? Have people always seen Christ in your actions? Are you more Christlike now or earlier in life?

After the resurrection, Jesus appeared to the disciples at the Sea of Tiberias (Sea of Galilee or Lake Gennesaret). They were fishing at night (cooler, fewer bugs), and they had a lot on their minds. What to do now?

In the early morning, Jesus was on the shore, and they didn't recognize Him. Maybe He didn't want them to, or maybe His appearance was different, or just maybe they weren't expecting Him.

Many times, when we aren't expecting Him, Jesus will come to us. And He doesn't come to our strength. For instance, if you're primarily a thinker, He may prick your emotions or feelings.

Jesus told His disciples to fish on the other side of the boat. When they followed Jesus's words, their nets were full. Maybe in your life, you're doing it the wrong way. First, you aren't sure who He really is, and second, you are fishing on the wrong side of life!

He invited his disciples to come and eat. He had a fire, fish, and bread, and even though we don't know where they came from, we do know Jesus will provide all that you need (I didn't say "all you want").

By the way, John 21:11 is specific in the number of fish caught: 153. That was the number of known languages at that time; everybody can have a relationship with the greatest Fisherman in history!

Keep your eyes open this week and look at people differently; be open to the presence of Jesus in different ways. Maybe it's time you met the Risen Christ in a way you never expected. Maybe you have met Him but just didn't recognize Him in the needs of others.

That small inner voice that is persistently calling you to do something? Probably not Jesus, you say. But if it lifts up Christ's work now, there's a good chance it is!

Will anyone this week see Jesus in your actions, and if not, why not?

ILLUSTRATIONS

A pastor and his family were on vacation traveling down the highway when they saw a suitcase fly off the top of a car going the opposite direction. They stopped to pick it up, but the driver of the other car never noticed or stopped. The only clue to the driver's identity was a twenty-dollar gold piece inscribed, "Given to Otis Sampson at his retirement by Portland Cement Company."

After extensive correspondence, Otis was located and contacted. He wrote a letter telling them to discard the suitcase and all its contents and send only the gold piece. Mr. Sampson used the phrase, "My most precious possession," several times to describe the gold piece.

The pastor sent the gold piece and wrote a cover letter telling Otis about his most prized possession, Jesus Christ. A year later, the pastor received a Christmas package. In it was the twenty-dollar gold piece. Otis wrote, "You will be happy to know we have become active members of a church. We want you to have this gold piece. I am seventy-four, and my wife is seventy-two. We want to thank you, for you are the first one to tell us about Jesus. Now He is our most prized possession."

We never know how a simple invitation to someone could turn their life around. Would you be bold and ask God to give you such an opportunity?

* * * * *

There is a documented story about a man named Floyd. According to the standards of the world, Floyd was nobody. Floyd traveled around the country looking for work at harvest time. Floyd had no home and no place to go. A couple invited him into their home and gave him a home-cooked meal. Early the next morning, Floyd returned to the house on his way out of the town to thank the couple for the meal.

The wife, Jean, on impulse, wrote him a letter telling him of God's love. Then she tucked it with a little cash into a New Testament. She found his backpack in the yard and tucked the packet inside. This Christian couple never saw Floyd again.

Four years later, Floyd's sister wrote to them telling of his death. As Floyd's sister was going through his few belongings, she found the New Testament, its pages soiled with use, and the letter from Jean which told of God's love. "They must have been very dear to his heart," the sister wrote, "for he carried them with him until he died."

It was such a simple gesture—a note, a small Bible, and a little cash—but surprise, little counts for a lot when you are doing the work of the kingdom of Jesus the Christ. Would you be bold enough today to pray for the opportunity to bring someone closer to Christ? To ask in prayer that you be given the chance to make a meaningful difference in a person's life.

* * * * *

Dr. Harry Ironside used to tell a story about a group of dissidents who left a church to begin what they hoped would be the perfect church. The new congregation considered themselves to be such a spiritual blessing to God that they put a sign outside their church: "Jesus only."

The church didn't reach out to the community; they only ministered to themselves. One day when Dr. Ironside went by the church, he noticed the first three letters, "JES" had fallen off their sign to reveal a new message, "US only!"

The new message revealed the truth about that church's ministry. The Christian is called to look outward, not only as a church but also as an individual Christian. Were you on the outlook today for opportunities to be of service?

* * * * *

WHO ME?

And the Lord said, "Go."
And I said, "Who me?"
And He said, "Yes, you."
And I said, "But I'm not ready yet, and there is company coming, and I can't leave the kids, and you know there is no one to take my place."
And He said, "You're stalling."
And the Lord said, "Go."
And I said, "But I don't want to."
And He said, "I didn't ask if you wanted to."
And I said, "Listen, I'm not that kind of person to get involved in controversies. Besides, my family won't like it, and what will the neighbors think?"
And He said, "Baloney."
And yet a third time, the Lord said, "Go."
And I said, "Do I have to?"
And He said, "Do you love me?"

154

And I said, "Look, I'm scared. People are going to hate me. And cut me up into little pieces. And I can't take it all by myself."

And He said, "Where do you think I'll be?"

And the Lord said, "Go."

And I sighed, "Here I am; send me."

* * * * *

I share with you an incident that happened to me in 1990 before my call to pulpit ministry. Two friends and I were walking across the capital grounds in Richmond during lunch break when a man appeared walking beside us. He looked a little disheveled and asked for some money for a meal. It was something about his eyes, his demeanor, and I wanted to help, but my intellect took over, and I didn't.

One of my friends gave him some money, and we walked on. My friend then stopped and said, "I'm going to find him and give him some more money," and he went in search of the man.

Later, I saw my friend in an adjacent office, so I asked him how much money he gave the man. He replied, "It was the strangest thing. I couldn't find him; he just disappeared even though the streets were wide and empty."

Our Lord said, "For I was hungry and you gave me nothing to eat, I was thirsty and you gave me nothing to drink, I was a stranger and you did not invite me in, I needed clothes and you did not clothe me, I was sick and in prison and you did not look after me" (Matthew 25:42-43).

There are still times when I have opportunities to respond to requests, and I try to keep an open heart for, at the end of that day, I felt that this was a Christ-moment, and I didn't act, and I still remember it to this day. The Risen Christ will give me an opportunity, or act through me, to provide a service in His name. Many times, He comes to us in areas where we are not so strong. If we are great thinkers, He will touch our hearts with a strange emotion to reach out. We want to, but then we think, "What is he going to do with the money?"

Jesus never asked, "What are you going to do if I heal you?" He just healed the person.

I plan to be ready the next time. The person will see Christ in me.

PRAYER

Dear heavenly Father, Lord of Creation, Provider of love and all things good, receive my humble adoration for You. I gather in praise seeking to walk proudly and reverently as Your child, created in Your spiritual image. I know of Your presence through the Holy Spirit, but I am still mindful of the times I elect to act independently of Your counsel. But I pray that I may be given a new purpose—to minister to my immediate family by inviting these loved ones to worship You in family grace at mealtime, general prayer, Scripture reading, and Sunday worship, and by setting the example of one who does not just talk the talk but also walks the Christian walk.

I know that these days, the force of darkness has, and uses, many weapons to weaken my family unit. Let all know that through a close relationship with You, we all may come to trust and have faith in Your ways, knowing that in this way our family will be strengthened. As in our prayers we call You "Our Father," help each one of us see that Your ways are to our benefit, Your wisdom above ours, and Your loving presence always available to each of us. Come upon each family member in the presence of Your Spirit and lead them to know that nothing is too great for Your strength, that peace can be ours during our earthly journey, and that the joy of Your heavenly home, promised by Christ, will one day be real.

Within my family and friends, Dear Father God, there are needs to be met so that wholeness may take place. May those I have lifted up by name in my heart see You as Father, to be trusted— may Your grace empower them with healing of the mind, body, and spirit. For the unrest in our country, may the teachers of hate be silenced. May each heart and soul live as "One nation under God."

May the ways of Jesus the Christ grow stronger in my life as well as in the lives of other Christians. May my example lead others to see faith in action. These things I ask in the precious name of Jesus the Christ who taught the prayer saying, "Our Father . . ."

Where Are You Going to Shop for Answers?

SERMONETTE

Romans 1:18-32

Would you go to a grocery store to buy a new lawn mower? When you want to purchase something, you need to know where to find it. And if you don't have a clue, now there are search engines, or you can just ask somebody as they did in Jesus's days. Once you reach out to "information companies," you will be bombarded by people trying to sell you their product.

The Apostle John (son of Zebedee) wrote the books of John and Revelation and gave us these words, "Do not love the world or anything in the world" (1 John 2:15). There goes your favorite steak!

Most theologians believe John was referencing the world of sin. Anyone who watches news on TV or reads the paper knows that sin is in the world. It's an opposing force to God's love, saving grace of Jesus, and the presence of the Holy Spirit. Sin versus God's way through Jesus and the Holy Spirit—both shops are open 24/7.

The devil's presentation is very glitzy, and he's going to appeal to greed, lust, fleeting happiness, gossip, and other destructive things. (The world is your plaything; get all you can any way you can; it's all about you!) Forget service, helping others, discipline, and eternity—live it up. Besides, some evil might just spice up life, like an affair!

Where are you going to shop? Jesus says, "No one can serve two masters" (Matthew 6:24).

John continues the thought in verse 1 John 2:15, "If anyone loves the world, love for the Father is not in them." Verse 17 says, "The world and its desires pass away, but whoever does the will of God lives forever."

In the world, you buy mainly with your eyes. Concerning the Kingdom of God, you buy mainly with your heart. When you shop in God's store, you look and use (1) Prayer, (2) Scripture, (3) Worship, (4) Belief in baptism, (5) Repentance, (6) Grace, (7) Resurrection of Christ, and (8) Our heavenly home.

The way of sin offers (1) Prejudice, (2) Hatred, (3) Hurtful behavior, (4) Manipulation, (5) Racial slurs, (6) Gender attacks, etc.

When situations in life are presented to you and information is needed to come up with the correct answers, the question becomes, in which store are you going to shop? The devil is hoping you will at least shop in both!

ILLUSTRATIONS

In a play by Elie Wiesel, Berish the innkeeper and his daughter who has been emotionally damaged by the slaughter of her friends and family are speaking in the inn. Berish has just come in, and he yells at Marcia, "Don't tell me what to do. You're getting on my nerves; the whole world is getting on my nerves!"

She responds, "Then you better get yourself another trade, mister. Better yet, get yourself another world."

There are times when things "get on our nerves." And we have three responses we can make. First, do nothing and continue to be frustrated. Second, change the situation and the causes of our frustration; many times we find these are out of our control. How do you change an irritable boss? The third is to change ourselves. No one can make you angry; you have to choose to get angry. For someone to put you down, you have to believe what they're saying.

We have to learn how to let the Spirit of God embolden us. When someone puts you down, a good response would be, "I'll take that under advisement. By the way, you sure look great today!"

Why fight the battle which they are so good at? And let's not take things so seriously! There's only one thing which should be taken really seriously—are you going to get to heaven?

* * * * *

A child had been selected to be the angelic messenger in the annual Christmas pageant. He had learned his lines, or so the teacher thought. But on the night of the pageant, the child panicked and just stood there. "Behold, I bring tide . . . Behold, I bring tide . . ." That was all he could manage to say. Then, looking over at his pastor who was beginning to fidget and at his parents who were a bit embarrassed, he blurted out, "Boy! Have I got good news for you!"

Our good news is that when we repent and accept Jesus as Lord and Savior in our life, God through the Holy Spirit can make a change in us. You might say, "But I don't want a change. I have made my life good—house, car, boat, hound dog, kitchen appliances, etc., etc., and I'm comfortable just as I am."

Are we to take our resources, time, and energy and hoard our material things? Is your good news, "Look at what I have" instead of "How can I serve"?

It might be a good idea for us all to start writing the speech we're going to give to Jesus when we stand face to face one day. Are the words going to flow, or are the excuses going to stick in our mouths?

* * * * *

A Philadelphia legal firm sent flowers to an associate in the Baltimore area upon the opening of her new offices. Through a mix-up, the ribbon on the floral piece read, "Deepest Sympathy." When the florist was duly informed of the mistake, he let out a cry of alarm. "Good heavens," he exclaimed. "Then the flowers that went to the funeral said, 'Congratulations on your new location.'"

160

Jesus never described heaven; I believe He knew words wouldn't come near to describing such a place. But Jesus did say we should be willing to do whatever it takes to make sure we get there—it's that fabulous! It's never too early to start planning for a trip.

One day, each of us will make a trip to be in God's presence. We're told in Scripture that this earthly journey is not our final resting place. We're just passing through to our eternal home. And when you become aware that your last day on earth will happen, you also know that one day your departure could be very swift. So the question becomes, how do you prepare?

Some years ago, I agreed to take a friend to the airport. I remember picking him and his four large suitcases and two duffle bags up, and I wondered just how long his trip was to last. I was very surprised when he told me—one week!

When you start preparing for your journey to your final home, how many suitcases will you be able to take? Well, obviously the answer is none. Your possessions, money, and even your reputation/prestige will be left behind. You can pack the generosity you have shown, especially to the lost, the least, and the lonely. Also, your acts of love and charity. The only things you'll be able to take with you are those actions taken through your relationship with the Risen Jesus the Christ.

One thing is certain—you will make the trip. Before it's too late, now is the time to ask yourself, "How's my preparation coming along?"

In the last century, an American tourist paid a visit to a renowned Polish Episcopal bishop. The American was astounded to see that the bishop's home was only a simple room, containing books, a table, and a cot. The tourist asked, "Bishop, where is your furniture?"

The Bishop responded with, "Where is yours?"

The puzzled American said, "But I'm only a visitor here; I am only passing through."

The Bishop replied, "So am I; I too am just passing through."

If we made a list of the things which we absolutely could not live without, I feel it would be a small list. We choose things over service, getting more over giving more. I wonder why we do this?

* * * * *

A middle-aged woman had a heart attack and was taken to the hospital where she had a near-death experience. Seeing God, she asked, "Is my time up?"

"No," God replied. "You have another forty years to live."

Upon recovery, the woman decided to stay in the hospital and have a facelift, liposuction, and a tummy tuck. She even bleached her hair blonde; figuring she had these years left, she might as well make the most of them.

After being released from the hospital, she was crossing the street when she was hit by a car and killed. When she arrived in front of God, she complained, "I thought you said I had another forty years! Why didn't You pull me out of the path of that car?"

God replied, "I didn't recognize you."

PRAYER

Dear God of inspiration and love, I have a new day, and I thank You for Your Spirit which watches over me. I do not know what joy or sorrow will find me, but Your presence, strength, and grace are sufficient for my needs. I am especially mindful today of those who are no longer with me but now reside in Your heavenly home. Memories live within me for each one who journeyed with me in life even if for a short while. May they be enjoying peace, rest, newness of spirit in the company of the saints, and overwhelming excitement in the presence of the Risen Lord and Savior, Jesus the Christ. May my reflection on their lives instill within me the commitment to lead my life in such a manner that I will also take my place with You when my earthly journey ends.

Christ came, suffered, and died that I might have life eternal; open my heart to His ways. May I come to fully understand that my purpose in all I do is to worship You by my words and actions. I accomplish this by service over self, humble not haughty ways, and love without judgment in place of hate and denial.

Lord, I come as an imperfect person, but I strive in the desire to be faithful and place Christ on the throne of my very being. Guide me to understand that nothing in life is more important than my relationship with You through the saving grace and acceptance of Jesus the Christ as Lord and Savior. May the promise of eternity with You guide me during the span of my earthly years.

Dear God, some of my family and friends, as well as myself, struggle with difficult days. May each of us grow closer to You even in adversity, for You are the God of hope and restoration. Let no fear separate me from You.

I continue to lift up this world where hate and intolerance continue to thrive. Convict the hearts of leaders to seek peace, compromise, and unity. Strengthen Your faithful followers in the resolve to seek Your way in all things.

These petitions I make in the Precious name of Jesus who taught the prayer saying, "Our Father . . ."

Easter Reflection

SERMONETTE

Mark 16

As we travel along on our earthly journey, we discover at an early age that life contains many different seasons. The ones most noticeable are the predictable changes in climate conditions such as spring, summer, fall, and winter.

Later in life, the seasons of childhood, youth, adulthood, and senior citizen bring different challenges. We discover that our abilities change and ole "use-ta" has a great effect on our lives. But nothing is as profound as the seasons found in the gospel good news story of Jesus the Christ.

The birth, ministry, death, and resurrection of our Savior not only touches our life now but provides the path for our eternal salvation. The very presence of God coming to live in human form; the example set in a ministry of service; the agonizing death on a cross to bear the sins of the world, including ours—these acts of grace and sacrifice give us the great example of love. However, the story wouldn't be complete without the season of the resurrection story. For here we find our hope and joy that one day we will conquer death, as Jesus did, and we will enter God's Kingdom as our final resting place. We truly take Christ at His word when He said, "I am going there to prepare a place for you" (John 14:2).

Because they found His tomb cut from solid rock was empty, we are now able to say, "He lives, He lives!" Our Savior has risen indeed and will welcome us into His arms one glorious day. Easter is the season that turns the darkness of despair into real hope of a glorious eternal life.

The resurrection story is not just about Christ waiting for us. We also see that the Risen Christ, with the Holy Spirit, is available to guide us on our earthly journey, give us the desire and strength to seek Christlike behavior, and courage to testify to our faith by our words, deeds, and actions. If we will walk in truth and faith, they will lead and strengthen us to defeat any fear, apathy, excuse, or disunity which could cause us to lose our purpose.

May we be energized by the resurrection story and never let fear keep us from God's vision. May the Easter season bring you great joy and comfort as your soul drinks in the event that changed history forever. May the seasons of your life be in sync with the spiritual seasons of our Christian faith. He Arose; He Arose; Hallelujah, He Arose!

ILLUSTRATIONS

We never know when we will make our trip to our eternal home.

Two men were avid baseball fans; you might say they were fanatics. They got into a discussion one day about whether or not there was baseball in heaven. So, they made a pact that if one died before the other, the one would find a way to communicate from the great beyond and tell the remaining friend what to expect.

Sure enough, one of the friends died and prevailed upon St. Peter to let him notify his living friend that there was indeed baseball in heaven. He could say nothing else, but he did appear to his friend in a vision. He said to his friend, "As to our discussion about baseball in heaven, I have good and bad news. The good news is that yes, indeed, there is baseball in heaven. The bad news is that you're pitching tonight."

* * * * *

One Christian decided to take a shortcut in reading the Bible. He decided to use the "open window" approach. He put his Bible by a window and let the wind blow the pages, and he quickly put his finger on a verse. The first verse he pointed to read, "Judas went and hanged himself."

Not a very good verse, so he did it again. This time he put his finger on the verse that read, "Go do thou likewise."

Finding these unacceptable, he did it a third time, and the verse read, "Whatsoever thou doest, do quickly."

* * * * *

The pastor of the church I formerly attended told this story.

During a dream I had last night, I died and promptly met with St. Peter at the famous Pearly Gates. Upon being taken into heaven, St. Peter began to show me around. One immediate observation I made was that on the walls of an enormous warehouse, I saw thousands of clocks. All of these clocks were ticking away but at different rates. I then noticed that under each clock was a nameplate with a name engraved on it. Naturally, I asked the significance of all of this. St. Peter informed me that each clock was designed to keep track of an individual still on earth. Each time the person represented by the clock committed a sin, the hands on the clock made a complete revolution. Upon closer examination, I began to recognize a few names. After searching for Les Goode's name and not finding it, I inquired as to the location of his clock.

St. Peter replied, "Oh, his clock! Well, we moved his clock into the office and are using it as a fan!"

* * * * *

A little boy met a man who was lost on a country road. The man stopped his car and asked the boy, "Son, do you know where Fairview is?"

The boy said no.

The man said, "Do you know where Interstate Forty is?"

The boy said no.

"Then do you at least know where the intersection of Bear Road and Squirrel Hollow is?"

"No," the little fellow replied.

"Well," the man said, "you are about the most ignorant person I have ever met. You don't know much of anything, do you?"

The small boy replied, "Mister, I do know one thing; I ain't lost!"

If you find yourself going in different directions trying to find peace and joy, could it be you have lost God's path? If we don't stop and pray about it, is it possible for us to be going in the wrong direction and not even know it?

* * * * *

Several episodes in the Bible involve Jesus and children.

Eight-year-old Dustin was discussing parent problems with his friend. Of course, they had lots of complaints. Dustin was overheard complaining, "First they teach you to talk, then they teach you to walk, and as soon as you do it, they holler, 'Sit down and shut up!'"

* * * * *

Many people don't seem to understand that all actions have consequences. We hope the consequences are good, but sometimes, they aren't so good because we didn't fully think out what the results could possibly be.

An eight-year-old was seated at the dinner table with her parents and grandmother on her mother's side. The grandmother asked the eight-year-old to please pass the salt. She refused.

Her grandmother reasoned with her. "My food will taste better with salt. You want your grandmother to enjoy her meat and potatoes, don't you?"

The little girl still refused to pass the salt. At this point, the mother leaned forward and said, "If that salt isn't passed to grandmother now, I am going to spank something, and it is not going to be the saltshaker!"

And when an action's result is bad consequences, it's very hard to accept responsibility. Rather, we often try and put the blame somewhere else. Our attitude seems to become, "It wasn't my fault."

When God asks us one day why we didn't fully worship Him regularly, who will we blame it on?

PRAYER

Dear God, as I come to proclaim my loyalty to You, I first must admit that some of my thoughts, deeds, and actions or inactions have not been showing such loyalty but rather a loyalty to my selfish desires. I find myself like the Apostle Paul who felt there were times when he didn't do what he wanted to do or did things he didn't want to do. I beseech Your forgiveness for the times I lapsed into self-serving behavior. Give me a clear vision that I might not repeat my shortcomings.

Your forgiveness to a truly repentant heart is certainly one of my greatest blessings. For as I continue my earthly journey and strive for—but will not reach—perfection, I know that even when I deviate from the path of Christlike behavior, You will hear my prayer and restore me to the presence of Your love. Your presence through the Holy Spirit enables me to find peace, hope, and joy now and to bathe in the glorious understanding of my eternal presence with You one day in the heavenly realm. Your ever-present presence in my life enriches me now, and the promise of my eternal home gives comfort, peace, and a sense of excitement that one day I will also be in the very presence of Jesus my Savior and the saints who have gone before me.

Although I often get caught up in the earthly race of judging my wealth by material possessions and money in the bank, may I more fully come to understand how rich I am by Your presence in my life now and the end of my earthly journey. Guide me to spend more time preparing my soul and less time accumulating more things; less time being wasteful while many have nothing; and more time seeking ways to serve. May I begin to see my wealth not so much as in dollars but rather in devotion to You.

Place upon my heart how to seek joy in giving, serving, and uplifting those around me, allowing them as well as myself to know and use gifts and talents to seek ways to worship you as the driving force for my life. Strengthen world leaders and righteous men and women to resist evil ways. And may comfort and peace be found by our loved ones and others who may be suffering. In their trials, may a new relationship be forged with You. These things I ask in the name of Jesus the Redeemer who taught the prayer saying, "Our Father . . ."

The Word Is "Persevere"

SERMONETTE

James 5:10-12

Jesus and the disciples knew of storms. The disciples were with Jesus in a boat, and a storm was upon them; they were in panic mode. Jesus, the solid Foundation upon which we stand today, was asleep! "You of little faith, why are you so afraid?" (Matthew 8:26)

Storms of life can put fear in our hearts. But don't you know that storms of life can also be times of growth? When you have faith and trust in the Holy Spirit through Jesus the Christ, you will not only come out stronger, but you will come out peaceful, knowing a presence was with you. It will become certain in your very inner being that you never have to journey through a "storm" of life alone.

But don't expect to always come out of the storm immediately. You may have to go through steps one, two, three, and four (maybe even five!) to get out of the storm. And when you come out, you might not come out where you thought you would. But you will come out if you are strong in your faith—at the place the Holy Spirit has chosen—if you persevere in trust.

The devil wants you to act in fear and doubt and to give up. Jesus says to your heart, "Let's get it on!"

When Jesus knew He was going to leave us (be crucified), He told us the Father would send the Counselor, Protector, and Holy Spirit. Why do we try and deal with storms and various unhealthy situations by ourselves when we have this power of God available to us? Satan will always try to convince you to do it alone.

Imagine you feel called to two separate courses of action. There is a real tug-of-war, but time is up, and you have to decide. One course seems to center on your wants but does not include anything really bad. The other course tends to be more in line with God's love and the way of the Holy Spirit. How do you decide which course will help you become more Christlike? First, in prayer, ask for wisdom and the presence of the Holy Spirit to guide you. Second, apply the tried and true question—what would Jesus do? And when you feel or understand your direction (or maybe a new one), go for it and persevere with determination. But be ready to celebrate; it will change your life!

ILLUSTRATIONS

By the way you act, would someone say that you were a smart person? Not like the man who went mountain climbing with his friends. Just as they had scaled their way to the top, he fell over a cliff. His companions tried to rescue him. Ever so carefully they leaned over the cliff and yelled, "Ed, are you alright?"

Back came Ed's voice, "I'm alive! I'm alive, but I think my arms are broken."

"We will toss a rope down to you and pull you up."

"Hurry, hurry," cried Ed. When Ed was about three-quarters of the way up, it suddenly dawned on them that Ed had said he had broken both arms.

"Ed," one of them yelled, "if you broke your arms, how are you holding the rope?"

Ed responded, "With my teeeeeeth."

When you walk in God's way, people might not only feel you are smart, they might even feel you have wisdom. Praying to God, being guided by the Scriptures—they could be right. What do you think, or better yet, what do you feel?

* * * * *

Did you make any New Year's resolutions? Weight Watchers and Nutrisystem and all the other diet plans have their biggest month of the year in January. Regulars at the gyms are not dismayed with the large crowds in January and February, for they know it will be business as usual after that.

Did you hear about the notice that appeared in a church bulletin which read, "Weight Watchers will meet this Tuesday at 7:00 pm. Please use the large double door at the side entrance"?

Some have resolved to pursue an exercise program while others follow the reasoning of a fellow who said he didn't believe in exercise. He says if God meant for us to touch our toes, God would have put them further up on our body.

One man said his doctor suggested he try running in place. The man asked, "In place of what?"

Could it be that sometimes a program of good intentions is simply not enough? It's amazing how that same program, coupled with prayer, can result in a different outcome.

* * * * *

Once there was a child prodigy named Ana Maria de Bottazzi. Ana began playing the piano at the tender age of two. She gave her first piano recital in her native Buenos Aires at the age of four. She toured many countries. By the time she was eighteen, she had performed recitals throughout South America, Europe, Africa, and Asia. At twenty-three, she was a full professor for graduate piano students at the largest university in Tokyo. Then tragedy struck.

This gifted pianist was almost killed in an automobile accident. The doctors were honest; the damage to her brain was extensive. They told her she would never play the piano again. For years to come, she couldn't do anything. Ana Maria said of her long recovery, "I still had hope."

The doctors removed fifteen blood clots from her brain. She couldn't even pick up a plate. She lost coordination. During her years of long recovery, her mother told her over and over again, "What we are is God's gift to us. What we become is our gift to God."

Ana began to believe in herself once again. She began to imagine herself playing at Carnegie Hall. In her imagination, she saw the people giving her a standing ovation. After a long sixteen years, she finally did walk onto the stage at Carnegie Hall. She was tearful. She sat down at the piano and prayed. She asked God to help her. Ana Maria played the piano for two hours. She was totally immersed in the music, she told later. When she finished her last piece of music, she turned to face the audience. Two thousand people were clapping, giving her a standing ovation.

For a second, she wasn't sure it was really happening. It was exactly like her daydreams. When she realized it was real, she broke down and cried on stage. As she took her bow, she offered another prayer. "God, this is my gift to you."

Since then, she has given ten more concerts at Carnegie Hall. She has also played for government leaders throughout the world. Not bad for a woman who was told she would never play the piano again. God said to Abraham, "Is anything too wonderful for the Lord?"

The answer of course is no. By the way, what gift that God has given you have you dedicated to God?

* * * * *

I Said a Prayer For You Today

I said a prayer for you today and know God must have heard.
I felt the answer in my heart, although God spoke no word.
I didn't ask for wealth or fame. I knew you wouldn't mind.
I asked God to send treasures of a far more lasting kind.

I asked that God be near you at the start of each day
To grant you health and blessings and friends to share your way.
I asked for happiness for you in all things great and small
But it was for God's loving care I prayed the most of all.

* * * * *

During my first appointment, an elderly and somewhat invalid lady of that congregation told me how she used to be so active in church, serving on committees, and how now all she could do was to make a list of people on her heart each morning and pray for them during the day.

I asked her to please not trivialize that by saying "All she could do." What a ministry of works and testimony to her faith. She was a faithful disciple of our Lord and Savior, refusing to be idle, refusing to be self-centered, refusing to be just comfortable. How is your ministry coming along?

PRAYER

It's a pleasant time for me to be able to pause while living the experiences of life, dear God, so that I might recognize Your presence in my life. I live with a somewhat impatient attitude and a strong desire to have my way, and it's refreshing to acknowledge Your presence.

And yet, it is still difficult at times for me to truly pray, "Thy will be done," for if I'm quite honest, there are times when Your will conflicts with my will. In seeking Your will, there are times when it's uncomfortable for me to feel that You are asking me to reach out to someone who is struggling; it might be hard for me. What do I say? How do I pray with them?

To find Your will seems awkward. How do I handle this if we have different opinions? And loving God, if they do not do as I think they should, will I succumb to the temptation to withhold my love for them? Even though I know in my heart, even in my times of disobedience to You, Your love is never withheld from me. In Your presence, I confess my doubts and fears and pray for strength to overcome and always seek Your will, even though it might make me uncomfortable at first.

Give me the understanding that You will never ask me to do anything for which You have not prepared me. Let me feel strongly that, in prayer, my faith and desire to please You will increase. Drive fears away from me and create in me a longing to have You as my constant spiritual guest, relying on Your wisdom, guidance, and will to shepherd me through the snares of life planted by the evil one. As You are a God of peace, the evil one causes confusion and fear. As You call me to a sense of spiritual joy, the evil one leads to worry, apprehension, and unrest.

Heavenly Father, lead me to resolve to live in Your love, measuring my behavior by the life, teaching, and example of Jesus. Help me to be comfortable knowing that You give me, in Your time, that which I need, not necessarily what I want. In Your love, touch those lifted up to You in my heart. Grant them healing, recovery, and peace. Continue to stir the hearts of world leaders that they will seek Your way in governing Your people. These I pray to You through the mighty name of Jesus the Christ who taught the prayer saying, "Our Father . . ."

Looks Like a Withered Hand to Me

SERMONETTE

Matthew 12:10-13

Many years ago, our representatives gathered to pass a document to declare our separation from England. "We hold these truths to be self-evident that all men have certain unalienable rights."

Two of these rights pertain to truth and freedom. In this day and age, when the truth is what you want it to be, facts are "fake news," and freedom is taken for granted even though many have died so we may have it, how do we find truth and freedom? In the New Testament, Jesus begins many of His statements with, "I tell you the truth." In John 8:32, Jesus says, "The truth will set you free."

What truth and free from what? Jesus also said, "I am the way" (John 14:6). We find truth, peace, and fulfillment when our lives are dedicated to God through Jesus Christ with the help of the Holy Spirit. We are free when we know who we are and to whom we belong. Scripture tells us the shed blood of Jesus our Savior will keep our souls free and peaceful.

If your life is not complete, maybe you are missing Truth and Freedom. Once when Jesus went to the synagogue, He met a man with a shriveled hand. We don't know how it happened, but it kept the man from being all he could be. Jesus healed him. The story made me wonder what my "withered hand" would be; what was holding my spiritual growth back? Is it something like insecurity, jealousy, fear, or something else which keeps me from being all God intended?

176

A woman was asked about her daily routine She replied, "I am self-controlled in all things but one. I am moderate in all things but one."

She was asked, "What is the one?"

Her reply, "I lie!"

What is your "withered hand" that is holding you back or negatively affecting your life? Isn't it time to turn it over to Jesus and let healing take place?

ILLUSTRATIONS

There was a farmer who had three sons, Jim, Sam, and John. No one in the family ever attended church or had any time for God. The pastor and others in the church tried for years to interest the family in things of God but to no avail. In fact, they didn't even want a visit from church people.

Then one day, Sam was bitten by a rattlesnake. The doctor was called, and he did what he could to help Sam, but the outlook for Sam's recovery was very dim indeed. Out of desperation, the pastor was called and apprised of the situation.

The pastor arrived at the house and began to pray as follows: "O Wise and Righteous God, we thank Thee that in Thine wisdom Thou didst send this rattlesnake to bite Sam. He has never been inside a church, and it is doubtful that he has, in all his time, ever prayed or ever acknowledged Thine existence, nor ever talked to a preacher. Now we trust this experience will be a valuable experience for him and will lead to his genuine repentance. And now, O God, wilt Thou send another rattlesnake to bite Jim and another one to bite John and another really big one to bite the old man? For years, we have done everything we knew to get them to turn to Thee, but all in vain. It seems therefore that what we could not do, Thou has accomplished with the rattlesnake. We give You the glory and the praise."

As is often said, be careful what you pray for; you might just get it.

* * * * *

A mother and her small daughter were discovering the dolls in a department store. "What does it do?" the child asked about each one.

The mother answered, "It talks," or "It wets," or "It cries." The dolls were rather expensive, so the mother tried to direct the little girl's interest toward an ordinary one that was more reasonably priced.

"Does it do anything?" the child asked.

"Oh, yes," the mother responded. "It listens."

The little girl reached eagerly for the doll.

We all need someone to listen to us.

Harpo Marx never went very far in normal schooling. Yet, he was welcomed in some of the most sophisticated circles. Someone asked him how he had managed to survive among the wits and the intellectuals of the Thanatopsis Poker Club and the Algonquin Round Table.

"Very simply," said Harpo. "They had to have someone to listen."

We all need someone to listen—not solve, just listen.

There was a survey not long ago reported in the paper that indicated that 97 percent of the women surveyed wished for more "verbal closeness" with their male partners. According to the same survey, the most frequently cited cause of women's anger was, "He doesn't listen (put down the paper, cut off the T.V. or the computer)." Seventy-one percent of the women surveyed said they had given up and no longer tried to draw their partner into a conversation. We all need someone to listen.

* * * * *

A lady was shopping with her daughter. The crowds were awful. She had to skip lunch because she was on a tight schedule. Now, she was tired, hungry, her feet were hurting, and she was more than a little irritable. As they left the store, she asked her daughter, "Did you see that nasty look the salesman gave me?"

Her daughter answered, "He didn't give it to you, Mom. You had it when you went in."

What look is on your face? Could it be called, rightly, a "Christian look?"

* * * * *

A mature-looking lady had an appointment with a marriage counselor and told him flat out, "I would like to divorce my husband."

To this, the counselor replied, "Well, do you have any grounds?"

She answered, "Why, yes, we have almost an acre."

The puzzled counselor said to her, "You don't understand. What I want to know is do you and your husband have a grudge?"

The lady answered, "Actually we don't but we do have a nice carport."

At this, the counselor shook his head and said, "Ma'am, I'm sorry, but I just don't see any reason why you should divorce your husband."

The lady said, "It's just that the man can't carry on an intelligent conversation; he just doesn't listen!"

Do you guess God ever feels that way about us? God is trying to give us joy, or comfort, or direction, and we are so involved with our "solutions" that we miss His message. Sometimes we are so impatient, and the opposite has to happen for God to get through. And we get frustrated and feel God is not helping us when all along God is waiting for a peaceful moment so He can give us what we need. How do you think we could have a better conversation with God which could have great results?

* * * * *

"The boneless tongue, so small and weak,
Can crush and kill," declares the Greek.

"The tongue destroys a greater horde,"
The Turk asserts, "than does the sword."

The Persian proverb wisely saith,
"A lengthy tongue, an early death!"

Or sometimes takes this form instead:
"Don't let your tongue cut off your head."

"The tongue can speak a word whose speed,"
Says the Chinese, "outstrips the steed."

The Arab sages say in part,
"The tongue's great storehouse should be the heart."

From Hebrew is the maxim sprung,
"Thy feet may slip but never the tongue."

The sacred writer crowns the whole,
"Who keeps the tongue doth keep his soul."

I believe that in the words found in James 1:19-27, Christians have placed before them a measuring stick of their Christianity. To listen in a loving way. And when in doubt, to ask ourselves, before speaking, "Is this what Jesus would have me say?"

Jesus said, "But I tell you that everyone will have to give account on the day of judgment for every empty word they have spoken" (Matthew 12:36).

Let this be the day that each of us, in commitment to our Risen Lord and Savior, Jesus the Christ, become people who are quick to listen and slow to speak. Who knows, the spiritual life you save just might be your own.

* * * * *

What is discipline anyway? *Webster's Dictionary* informs us that it is "training that develops self-control or character." So self-control is a major part of self-discipline. Well, if self-discipline involves self-control, then it seems we have to decide what behavior we feel is good for us and what behavior is not good for us. And this brings up the idea of motives.

Is what you are doing done to serve God? To uplift someone else? To not just take but to also give back? When it's always about you, does that develop self-control and character? I wonder how many of us would act differently if we simply asked ourselves before acting, what would Jesus have me do.

PRAYER

Heavenly God, I come to You today to confirm my faith in You. During the past days, You have been ever-present with me, and I ask forgiveness for the times I was so preoccupied with worldly things that I forgot to include You. I live many times with an impatient attitude and a strong desire to have my way, and it becomes difficult for me to truly pray, "Thy will be done."

There are times I can honestly say I am aware Your Spirit speaks to my spiritual heart, and rather than being obedient, I look for reasons or simple excuses to satisfy my selfish desires. For in my honesty, I admit there are times when Your will conflicts with my will. I feel the desire to break my discipline of regular worship, of service, or other Christlike behavior, and I tell myself, "Only this one time."

Then another time comes, and it begins to get easier. Make me vigilant to understand that evilness around me knows that even a conscious, bad journey begins with the first step. I sometimes feel guarded in trusting You because I'm not sure where You will lead me. I feel unable to fully commit, to place my dedication to You above all else, for that means I will have to give up control and be guided by Your Spirit. And yet, when we have this time together,

You make me aware that even in my times of disobedience to You, Your love is never withheld from me. Your spiritual presence is with me, and when I feel I am carrying the burdens of life alone, You give me the insight to realize that I am the one who drifted, not You. Create in me a longing to have You as my constant spiritual guest. Give me the desire of Your ways. For I do know that in closeness with You I will be led away from sin and its effects on me, even how I act with others around me.

When I feel Your presence challenging me, give me the courage to ask, "What would Jesus do?" then to move forward in confidence as I seek Christlike behavior. Although trials in life will be put before me, You have the power to move me through them and come out stronger on the other side.

I bring to You loved ones and friends who are on my heart because they are having a difficult journey. I ask that as it is in Your will, grant them healing, the quietness of spirit, and a deeper faith journey with You. I lift up world leaders—instill in each a desire for peace and Your will. Strengthen righteous men, women, youth, and children to resist and overcome evil. These things I ask in the name of Jesus Christ, the Risen Savior, who taught the prayer saying, "Our Father . . ."

Is There Any Doubt?

SERMONETTE

John 20:19-31

Jesus came to the disciples after the resurrection, while one of them was missing (Thomas, called "Didymus" meaning "Twin"). They couldn't wait to tell him, "We have seen the Lord!"

Thomas, a Jew, had stood by Jesus even in dangerous times. John 14:2,3-6 tells of Jesus at the Last Supper. "I am going there to prepare a place for you. . . . You know the way to the place where I am going."

Thomas said to him, "Lord, we don't know where you are going, so how can we know the way?"

Jesus answered, "I am the way and the truth and the life."

Thomas is known as Doubting Thomas for he had to have evidence to believe. "Unless I see the nail marks . . ." (John 20:25).

What is your faith story? Have you come to the point where you can fully accept Jesus the Christ as Your Lord and Savior just on faith? Is your faith tied up in the need of facts and evidence or can you accept Jesus and all He stands for without tangible proof? Do these words of Jesus ring clear to you? "Blessed are those who have not seen and yet believe" (John 20:29).

Although we can find peace, joy, and hope now, through belief we can claim eternal life. Through our Lord and Savior, you are heaven-bound. But in the meantime, Jesus is saying to all disciples, "Peace be with you! As the Father has sent me, I am sending you" (John 20:21).

Sounds like there's work to be done, and we are a part of it. And Jesus knew the gathered disciples (others besides the Apostles) needed God's help to carry out the mission they had been given, so He breathed on them and said, "Receive the Holy Spirit." Thus, anticipating what would happen fifty days later on the day of Pentecost (see Acts, Chapter 2).

So, what does that mean to each of us? Are we all supposed to sell all we have, give it to the poor, and become missionaries in some foreign land? Jesus tells us we all have gifts and talents but they aren't the same. It's therefore important to find out what you are legally, morally, ethically, and spiritually good at. Then you have to ask, am I using these in a way to enhance the work of Jesus during my journey on earth remembering the words of Scripture, "From everyone who has been given much, much will be demanded; and from the one who has been entrusted with much, much more will be asked" (Luke 12:48).

And if you need some tangible act to convince you of the gospel good news story, take heart in the story of Thomas. He needed proof (or he thought he did). Jesus didn't scold him or run him off but simply appeared to him and said, "Come close and touch me."

But Thomas realized that he didn't need to place his fingers in the nail holes, but rather, he was overcome with faith as he simply said, "My Lord and my God," and acknowledged Jesus as Lord and Savior at this high point of faith in his life.

I have met some people who profess to need more concrete evidence but who then refuse to be on the lookout when such confirmation appears. Remember, Jesus can come to you in a lot of ways. Maybe needing proof is an excuse. If you haven't completely made up your mind about Jesus, then you can put off doing His work now. Can you pray, "Come to me, Jesus, and become more real to me"?

Is there some part of your spiritual journey which has you saying, "I wish I could (Fill in the blank, like visit, etc.) but I can't because (I might say the wrong thing, etc.)"?

184

But look out! If you pray that Christ will become more personal and show you what your work is, you are as good as on your way! Don't forget the Holy Spirit is going with you.

"Well, I don't know, preacher," you might say. "I'm comfortable, and this seems like some big changes."

Well, answer me one question. Knowing what you know about your life and knowing through Jesus you are heaven-bound—are you sure you are sure about that?

ILLUSTRATIONS

If all behavior is motivated, what generally motivates you? Service, greed, manipulation, fairness? Are you always motivated by self-interest?

A San Francisco executive posted signs which read, "Don't wait; do it now!" throughout his factory hoping to inspire employees, to motivate them to action.

Several weeks later, a friend asked him how the staff reacted. He said, "The cashier skipped with ten thousand dollars. The head accountant eloped with the best secretary I ever had. Three typists asked for a raise. The factory workers voted to go on strike, and the office boy joined the Navy."

So much for motivation! Some would say the motivation message was successful. It might not have been what the executive hoped for, but it did help people realize their dreams. Are you motivated by taking or giving? What type of self-behavior causes you to feel good about yourself? And once motivated, do you apply the "Jesus Test" before acting? Why or why not?

* * * * *

I'm reminded of that song they used to sing on the music show *Hee Haw* which said, "Gloom, despair, and agony on me. If it weren't for bad luck, I'd have no luck at all."

We've all faced those kinds of days; maybe someone today is faced with a situation that makes the words of the song very real. If not today, it's a good possibility that all your days on earth which remain will not be blissful, and some clouds will rain on your parade. It's like you know you're going to have a bad day when you wake up in the hospital, all bandaged up, and look up to see your insurance agent who tells you that your accident policy does cover falling off the roof but it does not cover hitting the ground!

Then we hear the comics say, "Don't bother telling people about your troubles. Half of them don't care and the other half figure you had it coming." Gloom, despair, and agony on me. So how good are you at taking things in stride? Or is your way of handling such things to first see who you can blame and then second, putting on an attitude of, "Why me?"

I hold out that a person of faith would be able to say, "Even in this, I trust God." To be able to say, "God will strengthen me to handle this and even use it to make a better day."

Next time disappointment comes your way, don't fall down. Just fall on God.

* * * * *

It is hard to forgive; let's get even! Two little brothers, Harry and James, had finished supper and were playing until bedtime. Somehow, Harry hit James with a stick, and tears and bitter words followed. Charges and accusations were still being exchanged as Mother prepared them for bed. The mother then instructed, "Now, James, before you go to bed, you're going to have to forgive your brother who said he was sorry."

James was thoughtful for a few moments and then replied, "Well, okay, I'll forgive him tonight, but if I don't die in the night, he'd better look out in the morning!"

PRAYER

It is with a humble heart that I recognize, most Benevolent God, Your grace and unlimited love. I find that this world is sometimes a hostile place with the stress of work, health, and even family. I can get caught up in spending a lot of time with things that don't seem to be going as I planned. But lead me even in those times

186

to a thankful heart, for through Your Spirit, You can use even unpleasant times to strengthen me and give me a better day if I would but only have complete faith and trust in You.

I want to be able to give thanks to You, not only in the joyous times but also for the strength and peace of Your presence in times when I am tested. I want to be thankful because You are with me in all seasons of my life. I want my heart to be gladdened as never before as I call to mind Your presence in the birth, life, death, and resurrection of Jesus. For in that Baby, You have given the hope of my salvation and the hope of my heavenly home.

God of kindness and mercy, when the dark shadows of evil in the world call me to despair, keep alive within me the light of hope. For even when I do not see the answer, You not only have the answer, but You are in the future, setting in motion those things which will make it happen if I walk in faith. It would be the evil tempter's celebration to rob me of my hope and to have me question Your love for me and Your power over darkness.

Let faith and trust rule within me. Dear Lord, in this country, as well as other countries where unrest has led to destructive behavior, give to all people a sense of community which will mitigate against such actions. Open all hearts to a sense of honest conversation with the hope of addressing such situations where Jesus warns that, "If a house is divided against itself, that house cannot stand" (Mark 3:25).

For those on my heart who struggle with various uncomfortable situations, let hope abide within them as well as the comfort of Your ever presence. For hope tells me of Your miracles, Your peace, and Your promise to take me to Yourself when my earthly race is finished. I continue my hope for world peace. Leader by leader, country by country, change hearts for the peaceful existence of all people. These things I ask in the name of Jesus who taught the prayer saying, "Our Father . . ."

Did You Pass?

SERMONETTE

Matthew 25:31-46

Living like a Christian is hard. Jesus, the living presence of God in human form, knew this. Even Jesus as a miracle worker didn't fit in with the establishment for He asked such things as "Why didn't you visit me in prison?"

A bewildered group of disciples asked, "When did we not visit You?" Better yet, "When were You in prison?"

Jesus replied, "When you didn't do it for one of these, you didn't do it for me" (my summary from Matthew 25).

To walk in His way, we have to be willing to give up certain things. Things such as false pride, harmful judgments, and most "shoulds" and "oughts." We have to act as if we know we aren't better than others in the sight of God, but we are different. Being a Christian in this world is challenging, but if done right, no one should have to ask, "Are you a Christian?"

The way you live your life will answer the question for them.

We are aware there will be a determination of who will receive the reward and be allowed to enter the eternal kingdom of the saved and who will be consigned to eternal punishment in hell. The basis for judgement will be whether or not love was shown. Our rewards in the kingdom are based on belief and service without thought of reward.

In John 25:34-36, Jesus tells how the righteous will be surprised when they are told, "Come, you who are blessed by my Father; take your inheritance, the kingdom prepared for you since the creation of the world. For I was hungry and you gave me something to eat, I was thirsty and you gave me something to drink, I was a stranger and you invited me in, I needed clothes and you clothed me, I was sick and you looked after me, I was in prison and you came to visit me."

So, people on the right (righteous) and people on the left (cursed into eternal fire) heard Jesus and both sides were surprised.

As you read the words of Jesus, how many of the boxes were you able to check acknowledging the service you have rendered for the righteous criteria listed? Remember this is a list of who gets to heaven and who doesn't. Jesus is saying, "If you are not righteous, you will not see heaven and you will be in a bad place for a very long time (eternity)."

When you look at your inner thoughts which drive your actions, could you possibly add them to the list provided by Jesus? We sometimes feel we're getting away with something because we have rationalized it to death and Jesus won't know. But, guess what? Surprise! It will be brought up when the Book of Your Life is read to you. There are at that time no do-overs. The question becomes, based on what you know about yourself, did you pass the test to be called righteous?

ILLUSTRATIONS

One of the most successful golfers in the world is a man named Gary Player. Born into poverty in South Africa, Player recalls his childhood as one of loneliness, pain, and adversity. His mother died when he was eight, and his father worked long hours in the mines.

"We were so poor," he says, "that I used to take off my shoes whenever I could so they would last until the next pair."

After years of practice, Player turned professional in 1953. He has won more than 150 tournaments and continued to earn large amounts of prize money in addition to the one million a year he made from product endorsements. Though he was successful, Player was careful never to forget the real source of his success.

"Golf is the talent God loaned me," he would say. "You have no idea how many times I get down on my knees in gratitude."

This attitude of thanks is reflected in the words of 1 Chronicles 16:34. "Give thanks to the Lord, for He is good; His love endures forever."

What would you like to thank God for in your life? Is now a good time?

* * * * *

A cowboy went to church for the very first time in his life, and he was enthusiastic about the experience. He was telling a friend what had happened. He said, "I rode up on my horse and tied up by a tree in the corral."

The friend said, "You don't mean the corral; you mean the parking lot."

"I don't know; maybe that is what they call it," he said. "Then I went in through the main gate."

"You mean the front door of the church," said the friend.

"Well, anyway, a couple of fellows took me down the long chute."

"You mean the aisle."

"Yeah, they put me in one of those stalls with some other folks."

"You mean a pew?" suggested the friend.

"Yeah, now I remember that's what the lady said when I sat down beside her."

* * * * *

I believe there were a lot of people healed, miracles performed, and spiritual direction given to many people during Jesus's ministry which were unrecorded. There were no witnesses.

The story is told of a judge who stared down at the case-hardened criminal and said, "Because of the gravity of this case, I'm going to give you three lawyers."

190

"Never mind the lawyers," said the defendant. "Just find me one good witness!"

It comes down to belief and the way you treat your fellow travelers.

* * * * *

A noted evangelist was speaking at two different churches in a large city in the same week. A reporter was present at the first service. After the sermon, the evangelist pleaded with the reporter not to publish in the local paper any of the stories the evangelist had used that night since he was going to use the same stories the following night at the other church.

The next morning, the reporter published an excellent review of the evangelist's message and concluded with these words, "Rev. Jones also told many stories which we cannot publish."

How about your unpublished deeds? Is that repentance I hear knocking on the door of your spiritual heart?

PRAYER

In the quietness which now surrounds me, I come to praise You, Dear God of might and tenderness. I have faced different experiences even these last hours, but now my focus is on deep worship. I admit there are times when I'm not sure of life's direction, for the emotional drain of what the world is bringing seems unfair and difficult. It's even more hurtful when family or friends let me down with unfounded judgment or harsh words.

In the murkiness of a dark time, You then find a way to break through in the beauty of Your creation—the vibrant song of a bird, the rainbow, the gentle breeze, the inner voice which speaks to us with words such as, "Trust and be prepared for a better day."

It's in those times I realize you have not deserted me, but I am experiencing a lack of commitment because I have drifted from You. I become aware of how I have allowed worldly affairs to consume my time which pulls my attention from Your loving blessings. Forgive me, everlasting God, as I still get caught up in earthly events, and for a period of time, I forget that I can absolutely trust You. Show me how unsettled times give opportunities for increased faith. To walk in courage knowing that You, most Benevolent God, will take even these and make a blessing for me if I walk in faith and patience. For I am a person of hope; a person who travels in the spiritual as well as the physical. I am striving to one day enter Your heavenly kingdom.

Help me feel that I am never alone; Your Spirit resides within me. Help me to boldly seek new ways to serve You with a Christlike servant heart. Challenge me with new ideas, thoughts, and opportunities. I know that You will never lead me to action without giving me what I need to succeed. For in doing Your will, I find my purpose, my peace, and my joy. Accept on this day, loving God, my commitment to walk closer with You, for my created purpose is to worship You by my words, thoughts, and actions.

I lift up to You my family, friends, and strangers who struggle in mind, body, or spirit. Suit a blessing to each one, as it is Your will. Give to them, as well as myself, the trust to always pray, "Thy will be done."

Speak to the hearts of leaders throughout the world, drawing them to a decision to seek Your compassionate and loving will as they govern Your people. Let the attitude of control be taken over by the desire for service. These things I pray to You today, guided by the Holy Spirit through Your love and the passionate example of Jesus the Christ who prayed the prayer saying, "Our Father . . ."

What Do You Think about a Free Gift?

Acts 1:1-5

In the Scripture, we find instances where Jesus tells the twelve disciples that He will have to leave them. However, He makes a promise that He will have God send the Holy Spirit as a gift to be a guide, advocate, and counselor. After Jesus's death, we have an account of how this was realized in Acts 2:1-13. We call this the day of Pentecost as it explains how the Holy Spirit explodes upon the scene.

Pentecost is now celebrated on the fiftieth day following Easter. The chosen disciples (Apostles) were all together, including the recently added Matthias who took Judas's place. The Holy Spirit came as a great wind and what appeared to be tongues of fire rested on each of them, and they were filled with the Holy Spirit.

There are other references to the Spirit, including "the Spirit of God was hovering over the waters" (Genesis 1:2); Mary "was found to be pregnant through the Holy Spirit (Matthew 1:18); at Jesus's baptism, "the Spirit of God descending like a dove" (Matthew 3:16); and Jesus said, "But the Advocate, the Holy Spirit, whom the Father will send in my name, will teach you all things and will remind you of everything I have said to you" (John 14:26).

So, what are the benefits of accepting this aspect of God called the Holy Spirit? Is this gift going to be more trouble than it's worth? That depends on how far you want to be from the influence of God. The Holy Spirit will "teach you all things," mainly as to how you should live your faith. As the "Spirit of truth," it will lead you to truth (John 16:13). It will provide you the ability to "receive power" to stand against evil (Acts 1:8). But wait, there is more!

In Romans 8:26, we read, "the Spirit helps us in our weakness. We do not know what we ought to pray for, but the Spirit himself intercedes for us through wordless groans," even to the point that if we don't know what to pray for, just be silent, and the Spirit intercedes for us. "The Spirit intercedes for God's people in accordance with the will of God." (Romans 8:27).

In Galatians 5:22, we find that when we place ourselves in reliance on the Spirit, we receive certain fruits: "love, joy, peace, forbearance, kindness, goodness, faithfulness." We also feel the peace that passes all human understanding as we feel more confident praying to God, in the presence of Jesus through the Holy Spirit. Even if you leave something out, the Spirit will cover you!

More parts of your prayer will sound like, "Help me by the Holy Spirit to be more (you fill in the blank)." When you become Spirit-led, you will notice changes. Rather than making fun of someone, you will surprise yourself by giving compliments. You begin to rely on the Holy Spirit for guidance and wisdom. I would never go into the pulpit without this prayer, "Lord God, let me step aside. Use me to speak to your people through the Holy Spirit."

As you become more aware of this wonderful gift, you will trust the Protector to guide you in wisdom to resist the evilness of this world which tries to separate you from God. And, when out of the blue, you are reminded to contact Aunt Mae, who you haven't reached out to in a long time, you can thank the Holy Spirit. The Holy Spirit is real. It's a gift from God to assist and guide us in fighting sin. It's to counsel and lead us in wisdom. The question is, "How can I get this Holy Spirit?"

Peter answers this in Acts 2:38. "Repent and be baptized, every one of you, in the name of Jesus Christ for the forgiveness of your sins. And you will receive the gift of the Holy Spirit." There are no other requirements; you don't have to buy it, speak in tongues, or do anything else.

Have you confessed your sinful nature, accepted Jesus Christ as Lord and Savior, repented, and received baptism? If so, you have been given the gift of the Holy Spirit. You already have it. Why not use it? If you turn down God's gift and refuse to use it, what does that mean? Does it mean you want your way and not always God's way? The Holy Spirit—what does it mean to you?

ILLUSTRATIONS

A young schoolgirl stepped up to a store counter and said, "Sir, I need some school supplies—some pencils, some paper, a loose-leaf binder, and some answers. Sir, I need a lot of answers!"

I guess if there was such a thing as an answer store, many of us would spend a lot of time there. Or maybe not, for we have the Bible which contains answers we need for a stressless, spiritual life, and we don't have the time to read it; how would we find the time to drive to the store?

* * * * *

How much is a word worth? Back when Rudyard Kipling was England's most popular writer, the word went out that his publishers paid him a dollar a word for his work. Some Cambridge students, hearing of this, sent Kipling one dollar along with these instructions, "Please send us one of your very best words."

Kipling replied with a one-word telegram: "Thanks."

The word thanks is indeed one of our very best words, worth much to the person who speaks it and to the person who hears it. We often take people and what they do for granted. Are you in the habit of saying thanks, especially to someone close to you? When was the last time you said it?

* * * * *

We have to put forth some energy to have the lovely life of a Christian. We are not saved by works, but to live the enhanced Christian life, we have to put something in it. The generosity of God does not absolve a person from effort. Life is at its noblest and best when our efforts cooperate with God's grace and plan.

Not like the story of a police officer who caught a bootlegger with a lot of jugs in his truck. The officer asked what was in the jugs. The bootlegger said, "Water."

The policeman didn't believe him so he opened one of the jugs and took a gulp. He said to the bootlegger, "This looks like wine, and it tastes exactly like wine, therefore, this is wine. What do you have to say for yourself?"

The bootlegger exclaimed, "Praise the Lord. He done it again!"

That's not the kind of effort we are talking about.

* * * * *

The story is told of the pastor who was new to a church and, one month after arriving, learned that a rumor had circulated about him. It said that he had taken his wife to a concert instead of a prayer meeting. He had bawled her out as they sat on the first row, then had marched her down the aisle.

He let the rumor circulate for a few weeks, then decided to spike it. During the announcements on a Sunday morning, he said, "The story is not true for four reasons. First, I wouldn't take my wife to a concert instead of a prayer meeting. Second, I wouldn't argue with her in public. Third, I wouldn't create a scene by marching her down the aisle while the program was still on. Fourth, and finally, I'm not married!"

Now I believe a lot of people would have been involved in spreading that story, and I wonder how many spent as much time spreading the gospel good news story? When you are given the opportunity to participate in gossip, how do you handle it?

PRAYER

Dear God of heaven and the universe, You have created me in such a manner that I have a desire to believe. In order to feel complete and at peace, I am called to acts of worship. For only in the true expression of accepting You as the force of love and goodness within my being can I realize the things that are important in my earthly journey which will prepare me for my home eternal with You, Jesus, and all the saints who have gone before me.

I offer a repentant heart for the times I did not heed Your calling through the Holy Spirit. I need only look at the lives of many others, including brothers and sisters in Christ, to see how blessed I am. And yet, the evil, sinister force of this world would have me take full credit or chalk it all up to luck. This force will try and use Your blessings and the peace of mind they give me to separate me from You. The tempter can have us worship our blessings and not You, the source of love and good, even to selfishness and self-aggrandizement.

Put upon my heart Your will for the fruits of my blessings. If I'm not vigilant, the blessings of peace, security, and leisure time can draw me from worship of You. Give me clear inner vision to see the temptations which are laid before me. Impart the desire to walk in Christlike behavior, and grant me strength through the Holy Spirit to stand firm on the principles of my Christian faith.

Ever-loving God, my earthly journey is sometimes made difficult by events, the actions of others, or my actions. And the apparent unfairness which happens in my life's journey would have me believe I am alone. Yet, the presence of the Holy Spirit soothes me, for I then see that peace can be found through faith and trust in You, that your grace is sufficient. Your strength will allow me to see how You will strengthen my journey and allow me to prevail on the path You have for me.

For my loved ones and friends who suffer in mind, body, or spirit, which I name in my heart, I ask for a special blessing of hope, peace, and healing, as You deem appropriate. Let me be open to share Your love with them, to share the story of my faith walk, and to minister to their needs as the Spirit leads.

Dear God, with all the conflict in the world I continue to lift up world leaders; draw them from anger and hate to Your purpose and continue to strengthen righteous people to resist terror and evil.

These things I ask in the name of Jesus who taught the prayer saying, "Our Father . . ."

Are You Good At It?

SERMONETTE

Luke 14:15-24

We have a story in Matthew 4:1-11 about Jesus being led by the Holy Spirit into the wilderness to be tempted by the devil. We also see in that story how the sinister one thinks he has an opportunity. Jesus is physically weak from fasting for forty days and nights when the devil comes to tempt Him.

The dictionary defines the word "tempt" as the attempt to "induce or entice as to something immoral." Our spiritual morals are attacked. The first thing we have to come to grips with is, if satan is willing and bold enough to take Jesus on, we know he will not hesitate to come against us! Also, you can count on the fact that you won't be tempted to do good, such as lifting someone up who is feeling down.

One of the interesting things about our body is how God placed a sense of conscience within us to see the difference between right and wrong. Your conscience is not God speaking to you—it's you speaking to you! The Holy Spirit pricks our conscience to let us know we have been tempted. Then the devil uses his favorite tool; he helps us rationalize. "One time won't hurt anything, besides, if we don't do it, we'll miss out on a lot of fun!"

And then we decide we want to do "it" and more rationalization sets in, and we drown out the pleadings of the Holy Spirit. The line between right and wrong becomes blurred or disappears. One of the things we glean from the story of Jesus's temptation is that He, like us, was not alone in this confrontation. Jesus was accompanied by the Holy Spirit.

Do you ever feel alone? Do you ever feel God doesn't care? If God cared, why doesn't God change these circumstances? If you ever feel this way, you were just tempted!! It could be that God is sending a message to you. "No. I'm not going to change your circumstances. I'm seeking to change you so that you will depend on Me for strength through the ever-present Holy Spirit."

There's no reason for you to feel alone, for as a baptized Christian believer, you have the gift of the Holy Spirit within you. As you read this biblical story, you will see that God didn't keep the tempter away from Jesus. Fact is, the tempter tried three times, and Jesus then said, "Away from me, satan!"

And satan didn't say, "Make me." No, he took one look at the strength of Jesus and the Holy Spirit, and he put tracks down! But, make note of the end of the story in the Luke 4:1-13 version. "When the devil had finished all this tempting, he left him until an opportune time."

The devil is persistent and will come back again and again. When we are aware of temptation, we see from the story that the sin is not thinking about it but acting on the temptation. The example Jesus gave us is that He did not debate with satan. When satan pointed out to Jesus that He must have been hungry and should, "Turn these stones to bread," Jesus didn't say, "Well, I am very hungry so maybe if I just turn one to bread, that should be alright."

Jesus didn't try and rationalize or give an inch. He said, "Man doesn't live by bread alone, but on every word that comes from the mouth of God" (rely on God for the provision of food and spiritual food as the Israelites received manna). End of debate on that point.

When the devil catches you at a time when you think you are so clever and cocky that you can take him on alone, here is the plain and simple truth—you just lost! You might even fall for satan's greatest lie, "God has left you alone."

Quite the contrary, we have faith in this: God made us in God's spiritual image; God came in Jesus that our sins can be forgiven; Jesus proclaimed a place for us in the heavenly realm; and God has protected our spirit during our earthly journey with the presence of the power of the Holy Spirit.

Don't believe the lie; lift your head high. We are Christians saved by the shed blood of Jesus the Christ and strengthened by the presence of God's own Holy Spirit. We are heaven bound! Pray for the Holy Spirit to lead; don't debate the issue —you won't win!

ILLUSTRATIONS

A pastor's small son was told by his mother that he should wash his hands because germs were living in all that dust and dirt. He refused and complained, "Germs and faith, germs and faith! That's all I ever hear around this house, and I've never seen either one!"

Satan will make it hard for you to find out about him also. He will make it so rosy that nothing could possibly go wrong. And when it does, he has another way to cover this up with another rosy idea. We know it as a lie to cover a lie; better to stick to the truth and the light, for it's much easier to keep things straight.

* * * * *

A visitor in a small rural church overheard an elderly gentleman teaching a Sunday school class of young people. That elderly man put it this way, "If you're driving down the road of life and you see satan standing by the road trying to catch a ride, don't you dare let him in, 'cause it won't be long until he'll want to drive."

Sometimes the excitement of living on the edge is very exhilarating. But when we place ourselves within arm's reach of evil, we will generally lose. The dark side has too many tricks, and our own rationalization is one of his best. If we got by with this, then let's just move a little closer to the edge, for we have shown we can handle it. Meanwhile, the tempter is just reeling out the rope

to the noose we are putting over our own head. Want to be safe?
Stay in God's court; the game is just fine there.

* * * * *

The following poem was written by an unknown child and is
entitled, "When Everything Goes Wrong."

When I start the day off wrong
By sleeping just a wee bit long;
When little Jimmy cries through the night;
The washer breaks and the sink's a sight;
When the house is wrecked by sister's bunch
And Daddy's boss comes home for lunch;
I spill the milk and burn the toast . . .
That's when I need God the most!

When nothing ever goes just right,
The faucets drip all through the night;
We can't remember the Golden Rule,
Even while dressing for Sunday school;
Our bills and payments send us writhing
On the day when the preacher talks about tithing;
When our lives are everything but bliss,
Can the Master come on a day like this?

O, yes, He comes and stands quite near,
Until we take the time to hear.
To hear Him say, "Let Me take your troubles now,
And show you why, the when, the how."
It is just the time when castles fall,
He came before as I recall;
And He spoke to me the kindest word,
"Please remember I'm the Lord,
And these petty things around you now

Are really mine to bear, you know.
For I have promised and promise ever,
I'll forsake you never."

Our burdens will not necessarily go completely away when we bring the Holy Spirit into our life, but they become lighter; we have help holding them up.

* * * * *

There was this man who, while at the horse races, was having a bad day. He was really having some bad luck, but below him he spied a priest giving some sort of blessing to a horse. Lo and behold, in the next race, the horse won. Again, he saw the priest administer the prayer to another. Again, the nag won. When the priest was spied giving a ritual to another horse by the name of "Sureshot," the fellow raced to the window, putting his last dollar on him. Sadly, the nag came in last.

The fellow then approached the priest and asked him what happened. "Son, are you a Catholic?"

"No."

"I thought not," said the priest. "You don't understand the difference between giving a blessing and administering the last rites."

* * * * *

I'm sure there are times when we feel almost out of control. Things to do, people to see, places to go; it sometimes appears that we aren't sure where we are going, and we have a tailwind pushing us faster than we want to go.

In all of our stress and confusion, we are asked to take time out, to spend some quiet time, to reflect where we are in our walk with Christ. Some focus in our life is leading us the wrong way. We use the word "sin" to label this behavior.

I'm reminded of the parishioner who intended to compliment the pastor on his fine educational sermon as she said, "Until you came, we never really knew what sin was!"

But recognizing the problem is not enough. We must then call on God's power to make a change (repent). Would you say that your spiritual walk with God is perfect? If not, maybe now is a good time to look for those changes.

* * * * *

A good example of lack of belief was recorded by Ken Davis in his book entitled, *I Don't Remember Dropping the Skunk, but I Do Remember Trying to Breathe*. In the book, he tells about his physics professor who made him teach the law of the pendulum. Basically, the law states that when you release a pendulum, it will swing out and never return past the point it started. Ken hit upon a great idea. He had the professor sit in a chair on stage, and then Ken unveiled a pendulum of weight-lifting disks that weighed 250 pounds.

Ken pushed the weight up to the professor's nose and said, "If the law of the pendulum is correct, this will return and stop just short of your nose," at which point he let the weight go after swinging it far to the right.

The weight moved across the stage, seemingly picking up speed. After it reached the midpoint and started for the nose, Ken reported he had never seen a professor move so fast in all his life. Ken's professor understood the law but was unwilling to put his nose to the test.

In scary times, are we willing to fully trust God?

PRAYER

Dear God, I present myself to You, acknowledging I don't always measure up to Christlike behavior, by going against Your will with my actions and inactions. Grant me forgiveness and the presence of Your Holy Spirit that I may not only be aware of my transgressions but also have the strength of Your Spirit to mend my ways using Jesus as my example.

I realize I have now come to a time of decision. Your Word tells me the only way I find peace that I seek is to realize that being a follower of Christ is a full-time commitment. Impart to me the discipline of weighing all matters on the scales of Christ's teachings. But, Loving God, I know that I must first decide if Jesus was truly who Scriptures say He was—Your presence in human form. For, if I accept Him as Lord and Savior, then I must decide how much and which parts of my life will I devote to You through Him.

Your Spirit will have me question my motives for living worldly behavior below the standards of Christlike behavior. In living a life of commitment, Your love will draw me into openness and not stereotypes, fixed ideas, and behavior. Your generosity may well lead me to service in Your name and not selfishness of a closed mind and self-importance. Christ's promise of eternity in His and Your presence will motivate me beyond disappointments and trials of my earthly journey. So, let my decision today be to accept the gospel good news of Jesus the Christ and the Holy Spirit, leading me on a path acceptable to You, so that one day I may earn the greeting from You, "Enter good and faithful servant."

Allow me to focus on the goal of peaceful living through trust and faith in You. Enter in a meaningful way into the lives of those who suffer or have not accepted Jesus the Christ as the path to You. I lift up a special prayer for those dear to me that their needs may be met, including spiritual comfort. And where evil actions take place in the world, unite righteous people in the cause of freedom in Your name. Strengthen those whose words and actions proclaim His teachings.

As I make my decision for faithful obedience, walk with me even more as I meet the coming trials of the world and any other temptations. These things I ask in the precious name of Jesus who prayed the prayer saying, "Our Father . . ."

No One Can Do This for You

SERMONETTE

Matthew 17:1-9

What a fantastic experience for the Apostles Peter, James, and John as they experienced the transfiguration of Jesus. They witnessed Jesus's face shining like the sun and His clothes were white as the light. Jesus had led them up a high mountain where they were joined by Moses and Elijah. They even heard the voice of God say, "This is my Son, whom I love; with Him I am well pleased" (Matthew 17:5).

These three men were terrified when they heard God. There was a sense of majesty and awe at the presence of God. The men threw themselves on the ground and Jesus, the caring one, came and touched them and told them, "Get up—do not be afraid."

In the transfiguration event, the three Apostles saw Jesus in His glorified state. No one else on the face of the earth ever had this experience. All the other people around Him formed their personal relationship only from what they were aware of in their dealings with Him. Some had heard Him preach or witnessed miracles; some people had only heard of Him, yet they believed!

Now the question comes to you. Since you didn't walk with Jesus and see these things or the transfiguration, why or why don't you believe in Jesus? We all know, just because someone in our family was a believer, it won't rub off on us. Your grandmother's/grandfather's/mother's/father's strong faith will not get you into heaven! Remember, God has no grandchildren! Some might say, "Well, I'm not sure; I'll do good works and maybe they will add up for a ticket."

Sorry, but works won't save you. You have to have a personal relationship based on what you experience and believe. And this becomes true to you in faith, even though you didn't walk with Jesus, witness the crucifixion of Jesus as salvation for our sins, or glory in the transfiguration event.

We accept in faith that the stories in the Scripture about Jesus are true. We accept that, at present, we are travelers with the Holy Spirit seeking Christlike behavior. We strive to grow in faith as we hope one day to have citizenship in heaven. And the question becomes, "Can I get there with a halfway approach? Will an acceptance of Christ in convenient times only do the trick?"

The answer will be seen in how your beliefs affect your present day-to-day living. No one should have to ask you if you are a Christian if they know you. If you act like a Christian, talk like a Christian, and walk the path of a Christian, you will be viewed as a Christian. Oh, by the way, if you're a mediocre Christian trying to walk in worldly and faith ways at the same time, they will know that also.

Our walk has to be different than the non-Christian. This doesn't make us superior to others, only different. We say a blessing over our food at home as well as in the restaurant. We lift up the people having a bad day with compliments. We lead in family prayer. In general, we show in all things that we hear a different drummer than do many other people. The Christian is transformed at baptism into the family of God, grows in acceptance of Jesus the Christ as Lord and Savior, and feels joyous about receiving the heavenly place in God's home. All of this without actually seeing God or Jesus and things like the transfiguration. But we accept it as truth. That, my friend, is what we call faith!

Jesus said to His Apostles, "Because you have seen me, you have believed; blessed are those who have not seen and yet have believed" (John 20:29).

One last point, the stronger you become in your Christian walk, the stronger you will appear to some of your present friends as you resist sinful ways. They might drop off! Remember, accepting Christ in your life doesn't make you superior, but it certainly will make you different. Good luck in showing yourself and others just how Christian you are!

ILLUSTRATIONS

Imagine, if you will, a wire stretched between two tall buildings, one on either side of the main street of a large city. And further imagine a lone individual standing atop the first building, announcing his intent to walk across the wire to the other side. Of course, a crowd has gathered below because what he intends is out of the ordinary. The tightrope walker asks the crowd if they believe he can make it across. They nod in approval. Carefully, slowly, but with assurance, he makes his way across.

Reaching the other side, he holds up a wheelbarrow and asks the crowd if they think he could push it across before him. Some nod in the affirmative. Some shrug their shoulders in response. The tightrope walker then singles you out in the crowd and yells down, "Do you think I can make it?"

Your response is yes, but then the walker says, "Then please come, prove your faith; ride in the wheelbarrow."

Christ calls us personally saying He will guide us through life with its dangers. Will you ride in the wheelbarrow of faith trusting Christ as your guide? It's one thing to say you trust Jesus—from afar. It's another matter to make it personal and commit your life to the care and guidance of our Lord and Savior!

* * * * *

Although we don't understand why we have to struggle, our faith calls us to believe that God will use it for our benefit. I'm reminded of a very recent story of a man who was confined to bed because of a lingering illness.

One day he noticed, on his sunlit windowsill, a cocoon of a beautiful species of butterfly. As nature took its course, the butterfly began its struggle to emerge from the cocoon. But it was a long, hard battle. As the hours went by, the struggling insect seemed to make little, if any, progress.

Finally, the man, thinking that the powers that be had erred, took a pair of scissors and snipped the opening larger. The butterfly crawled out, but that's all it did—crawl. The pressure of the struggle was intended to push colorful, life-giving juices back into the wings, but the man, in his supposed mercy, prevented this.

The insect wasn't like God intended. Instead of flying on rainbow wings above the beautiful gardens, it was condemned to spend its life crawling in the dust. That gives me the idea that God knows what God is doing, and often we don't. That's why we walk in trust and faith. It's a fact; you can depend on God, even when it seems the struggle is hard and meaningless.

Sometimes, to get from point X to point Y, we have to stop at A, B, C, and maybe even D. Even though it doesn't make any sense to us, we have to trust that God needs this to strengthen us and prepare us for Y. When we are faithful and keep the faith, we will receive the blessing.

* * * * *

It's our call to show every day how good a Christian we can be. I once heard a religious speaker say, "Live every day as if the archangel Michael was following you all day with a pad and pencil taking notes. Your best approach—take up the shield of faith which will extinguish the flaming arrows of the evil one."

* * * * *

Farmers in southern Alabama were accustomed to planting one crop every year—cotton. Year after year, they lived by their crop. Then one year, the dreaded boll weevil devastated the whole area.

The next year, the farmers mortgaged their homes and planted cotton again hoping for a good harvest. But as the cotton began to grow, the insects came back and destroyed the crop. The few farmers who survived decided to experiment the third year. They had the vision to plant something they had never planted before—peanuts. And, through peanuts, the farmers prospered greatly. Then guess what they did? They spent some of their new wealth to build a monument to the boll weevil—their adversary.

For if it had not been for the boll weevil, they never would have discovered peanuts. Even out of disaster, God can bring great delight. Next time something unpleasant comes your way, just go to God in prayer and ask for His vision. After a while, who knows, you might even want to build a monument yourself.

* * * * *

Reverend Rick Lemborg, pastor of First Presbyterian Church in Casa Grande, Arizona, describes himself as a Presbyterian by earthquake. He explains that his grandmother, a Baptist, moved the family from Iowa to California many years ago. A Presbyterian pastor visited her and invited her and the family to come to the Presbyterian church.

"I'm a Baptist," his grandmother said, "and it will take an act of God to get me to change and come to another church."

While they were chatting, an earthquake shook the home. Being from Iowa, she had never felt this and wasn't sure what it was, but when it was over, she told the preacher, "I'll join!"

Wouldn't it make faith a whole lot easier if God would give each of us some unmistakable sign? Perhaps not an earthquake, but some less frightening indication of God's interest in our affairs. Maybe He could write in the stars, "I am real!" or maybe write on the ceiling of our bedroom, "Believe in Me!"

I believe it was Woody Allen who said a million dollars deposited in a Swiss bank account would be a nice gesture. It would certainly seem to make it easier if each of us had our own personal, tangible proof about God. But, God's plan is that we have faith. Believing without having to prove it. Are you still trying to prove it?

* * * * *

A young woman was a kleptomaniac, and she decided to see a psychologist. "I would like to change," she told the psychologist. "I would like for you to help me stop stealing things."

After about a year, she was told by the psychologist, "I believe we now have your kleptomania under control, and you can go out in the workaday world just like everybody else."

"Oh, Doctor, I'm so grateful," said the woman. "I don't know how to repay you for your help."

"My fee is all the payment I expect," said the kindly analyst. "However, if you should happen to have a relapse, you might pick up a small transistor radio for me."

This psychologist knew something that we all know—change is hard for us, so faith can be also.

PRAYER

On this day, bountiful Father, I come to You with a sudden feeling that I need to spend more time in a House of Worship which You will lead me to. You have touched the hearts of so many before me who provided for places of worship, and I am truly grateful for their faithfulness. You have now placed upon my heart a new challenge that will further my fellowship among believers. May I, in faith and trust, follow the path You will place before me.

Lead me to commit to a living, viable church seeking to spread the gospel good news story of the Risen Christ. May my desire for service be nurtured in a fellowship of believers. Remove any and all fear and give me the peaceful spirit of knowing that all who labor in Your name do not labor in vain. May I be spiritually challenged to see new people and nudgings from You as opportunities to expand my spiritual life. What I have seen as the safe way of minimum participation has now stirred within me a need for a closer relationship with You in the company of like-minded Christians.

Going from the known to the unknown can be scary. However, if You have placed this in my heart, You will never call me to some form of worship without the present power of the Holy Spirit and the guidance of the Risen Lord, Jesus the Christ. The world will try and put roadblocks in my path to cause doubt, but if I remain faithful, it cannot quench the blessings You have for me with faithful trust. I know from Scripture that You will never ask anything of me without giving me the strength and means for success. Give me the courage to say in all matters, "God is in control; what does God want?"

For only then can I walk this earthly journey in the peace I desire. Strike my heart, dear God, to walk joyfully with You in all things, even new challenges. Look with favor upon my loved ones who need a special touch. May their faith uplift them.

I continue to pray that world leaders with hard hearts will be struck by the Holy Spirit and become more tolerant and supportive of their people. These things I ask in the precious name of Jesus the Christ who taught the prayer saying, "Our Father . . ."

Leftover Bits and Pieces

Two boys were walking home from Sunday school after hearing a strong preaching on the devil. One said to the other, "What do you think about all this satan stuff?"

The other boy replied, "Well, you know how Santa Claus turned out. It's probably just your dad."

* * * * *

Attending a wedding for the first time, a little girl whispered to her mother, "Why is the bride dressed in white?"

The mother replied, "Because white is the color of happiness, and today is the happiest day of her life."

The child thought about this for a moment then said, "So why is the groom wearing black?"

* * * * *

A little girl, dressed in her Sunday best, was running as fast as she could, trying not to be late for Bible class. As she ran she prayed, "Dear Lord, please don't let me be late! Dear Lord, please don't let me be late!"

While she was running and praying, she tripped on a curb and fell, getting her clothes dirty and tearing her dress. She got up, brushed herself off, and started running again. As she ran, she once again began to pray, "Dear Lord, please don't let me be late . . . but please don't shove me either!"

* * * * *

Three boys are in the schoolyard bragging about their fathers. The first boy says, "My dad scribbles a few words on a piece of paper, he calls it a poem, they give him fifty dollars."

The second boy says, "That's nothing. My dad scribbles a few words on a piece of paper, he calls it a song, they give him one hundred dollars."

The third boy says, "I got you both beat. My dad scribbles a few words on a piece of paper, he calls it a sermon, and it takes eight people to collect all the money!"

* * * * *

An elderly woman died last month. Having never married, she requested no male pallbearers. In her handwritten instructions for her memorial service, she wrote, "They wouldn't take me out while I was alive, I don't want them to take me out when I'm dead."

* * * * *

A police recruit was asked during the exam, "What would you do if you had to arrest your mother?"

He answered, "Call for backup."

* * * * *

"Preacher," said the chairperson of the Pastor-Parish Relations Committee, "I'm sorry to hear you are planning to leave us for another church."

"Oh, you have nothing to worry about," the pastor replied. "I'm going to recommend a successor who will probably be a better preacher than I."

"That's what worries me," said the chairperson. "Your predecessor told us the same thing!"

* * * * *

A young boy received a nice guitar for Christmas. He put his left hand on a fret and held it in one fixed position while he strummed on the instrument hour upon hour. His father became annoyed with him and said, "Son, you are supposed to move your left hand up and down the neck of the guitar to different frets and produce new sounds, like Chet Atkins and Les Paul, the great guitarists do."

The little boy replied, "Well, Dad, they run their left hand up and down because they are still looking for it. I found it!"

* * * * *

A Christian man died and was greeted by St. Peter. "Let me show you your new home," St. Peter told him. They walked past big, expensive, beautiful homes to homes that were moderate and finally to very small, tiny homes. The man said, "Why can't I have one of those nice, bigger homes?"

St. Peter answered, "While on earth, each time you do something for the Kingdom of Christ, you send up building material for your new heavenly Home."

Pointing to the very tiny house, St. Peter said, "This is all we got!"

* * * * *

A preacher was preaching a rather long, uninspiring message when he noticed a man on the first row of the church congregation had fallen asleep. The preacher tried to wake him by talking louder. It didn't work so he dropped his Bible with a bang on the floor several times. Again, it did not work. So he stopped and said to the man next to the sleeper, "Would you please wake him up?"

To which the man replied, "You wake him up. You're the one who put him to sleep!"

Acknowledgments

It is with loving appreciation that I give thanks to my wife, Renee, for the many hours she spent in organizing, proofreading, and submitting the work for publisher review. She offered valuable assistance in decisions to make last-minute edits to the text. With her understanding of Scripture, she was able to help in the discernment of spiritual implications found in the scriptural references quoted in this book.

I would like to thank Sarah Mason, typist, for her professional ability to transform my single-spaced, cramped efforts into a beautiful, easy-to-read product. Although she resides a long distance from Virginia, her understanding of the internet made communication between us effortless and allowed her to complete the project in record time. Her previous experience in typing such manuscripts was a valuable asset and helped us to forge a good working relationship.

I would be remiss if major credit were not given to the Holy Spirit of God for, first, enticing me to do this project and, second, for providing the strength, direction, and spiritual insight needed. There was always the feeling that someone was looking over my shoulder—I believe that was indeed the case! Concerning the contents of this book, I feel that I can confidently say with humility and love, "To God be the glory."

About the Author

Leslie "Les" Goode was born in Chesterfield County, Virginia, in 1941 and attended Midlothian High School. Upon graduation, he completed requirements for a B.A. degree from the University of Richmond, then entered the teaching field in Special Education in Colonial Heights, Virginia. In 1970, he was asked to join the Virginia Department of Education, Division of Special Education. While there, he attained a Master's Degree in Education and a Master's Degree in Administration. He served in this position until early retirement brought on by a very vivid and powerful "Word of God" with the instructions, "Feed my sheep."

After receiving a Master of Divinity degree, Les began the exciting and rewarding adventure of becoming a United Methodist country preacher. In 1995, he received the Excellence in Town and Country Ministries award from the Virginia Conference of Global Ministries, presented each year to one pastor who has demonstrated excellence in ministries.

Les is now enjoying many facets of retirement with his wife, Renee, in Williamsburg, Virginia. They may be reached at AGoodeCountryPreacher@gmail.com.